"Thus says the Lord, the God of Israel: Write all the words that I have spoken to you in a book, and call to Me and I will answer you and show you great and mighty things, fenced in and hidden, which you do not know."

Jeremiah 30:2 and 33:3

Contents

Foreword

In the scriptures we read of the many gifts which the Lord has placed within the body of Christ. This book is an example of one of those gifts; the gift of encouragement. I say this because this piece is a work that will meet you at your point of resignation from the faith and then it will revive you with the basics of discipleship and cause you to "press on toward the mark of the high calling of God in Christ Jesus."

Stephannie has taken the time to present to the Lord issues which many of us face. As a result of her *conversations with the King* we have the privilege to see where we have almost given up, why we were about to call it quits, and what it takes to keep the faith.

What is refreshing about her work is that she has traveled through the word of God, found persons and personalities, both familiar and not so familiar, looked at their plight with a scrutinizing, yet richly sensitive eye, and has extracted the necessary truths that transport our pain into power and our sense of victimization into spiritual victory. Indeed I am sure that you will find this compilation of meditations sound, profound, and perfect for day to day devotions. This book will empower you to persevere in your walk with Christ. It is my prayer that you would be blessed by God Himself as you read the encounters found within this book.

Rev. Carl J. Solomon, Pastor
United Baptist Church
Baltimore, Maryland

Preface

The Lord keeps all of His promises, one being that if we call on Him He will hear and answer us. His mode of communication varies from person to person as do our experiences with Him, still He speaks. Hearing His voice is an indelible experience. Knowing that He has something relevant to say about our lives is comforting, assuring, and totally awesome. His insights are doubtlessly significant to the whole person. Direction, instruction, peace, joy, understanding, eternal security, and other essentials for productive living are extended to us just from conversing with the King of Kings.

Although many Christians know how these blessings of God empower them, there remains an even greater number that find applying and connecting God's word to their lives difficult. The lack of divine knowledge, unexercised faith, and a quitting attitude are contributors to so great a number of defeated saints and delayed spiritual development. Burdened by the falling away from the faith, this compilation of meditative essays was conceived. To witness individuals dismiss accounts of God's mercy and grace in their lives and align themselves with worldly persuasions was disheartening to say the least. Greater still is my concern for those who are currently considering the renunciation of their faith to Jesus Christ. Having considered throwing in the towel myself, I know that Christ is able to show His followers the source and cause of temptations and troubles. My decision to remain in Christ has never failed me and remains to outweigh every alternative.

Conversations with the Holy Spirit have convinced me that His word is both preventive and prescriptive. The power of it binds undesirable outcomes that stem from misinformation and mistakes. Simultaneously, He releases divine essentials that can conquer and cure common ills. Yes, common evils. We are not passing through virgin territory. The Lord tells us that although some things seem new to us, they actually are not because there is nothing new under the sun, Ecclesiates 2:9–10; there is no temptation that is uncommon to us, I Corinthians 10:13; and the same sufferings are appointed to Christians throughout the world, I Peter 5:9. Although trials and tribulations are communal to believers and non-believers of the Risen and Reigning Lord, we have at our disposal good reports from a multitude of faithful witnesses. Successful sojourners of the past and sanctified soldiers among us testify of the victories found in Jesus. Every knee will not bow to and every mouth will not kiss the idols of this world, I Kings 19:18. We ought to be continually encouraged by yet another promise, that a great multitude that no person can number, Revelation 7:9–11, will share in a victory celebration over the evils of this world. What a mark of obedience.

Yet, in spite of God's good news and precious promises, people of God do think and have thought that their experiences are unique. Even the assurance that our God remains with us is doubted, Matthew 28:19. There is a prevailing thought that He abandons and forsakes His people especially in times of trouble. Such beliefs contribute to dependence in ungodly solutions and imperfect human wisdom. Thus, it is essential that we settle the Lord's assurances in our spirit so that we can experience all that He has in store for us.

I have learned that sharing the truth either encourages or incenses individuals. Nonetheless, it is God's will and my desire that every reader be blessed by the proceeding words of the Lord, particularly those who are in need of a spiritual incentive. In this book the Holy Spirit addresses some common issues that can either prevent or produce a favorable relationship with God and people. He also highlights some common mistakes made in the life of the disciple. He wants us to learn from mistakes, avoid and simply get over them. Although to err is human, He wants us to know that all mistakes do not have to be a part of our earthly experience.

I am thankful to the Holy Spirit for using this medium to give words of encouragement to those who have allowed their mistakes to govern their lives. He has something to say to the unweaned, discouraged, confused, and established believer alike. Thus, in keeping of God's nia (purpose), Conversations With The King has become a reality. For it is His nia that we delight in Him and certainly apply His word for spiritual prosperity as we walk with Him.

Persuaded to write promptly the report of the Lord, I pray that every reader believe and apply His messages. I believe that by His Spirit the perceptions of His people will be challenged and many of my brothers and sisters in Christ will experience spiritual and natural liberation.

May the passion of Christ prevail in your reading.

Stephannie R. Solomon

Acknowledgments

◆

Continually I thank God for the support of so many individuals, principally, my husband and daughter. From the inception to the completion of this compilation my husband has provided me with freedom and encouragement to write. Special commendations to my precocious daughter, Sierra Simone, who agreed to share me with the computer. Their patience, love, and understanding is a reflection of God within them.

◆

For the life of the late Dr. Samuel L. Banks, I thank God. His challenge to me to put pen in hand will never be forgotten.

◆

"Trust the Lord like you never have before Stephannie," helped to keep me focused during this most unique experience. Thank you Patricia Thomas.

◆

◆

The indefatigable acts of Marie Loving, Mary Demory, Vanessa Lang, and Barbara Barton truly confirm the gift of helps at work in each of them. Their support in preparing the manuscript contributed immensely to the fulfillment of its publication.

◆

The Lord has strategically placed individuals with fostering spirits and diverse spiritual gifts in my life. For each life I give Him thanks. From a myriad of acquaintances, I have received unstinting words of encouragement, wisdom, and knowledge regarding this written endeavor. I am beholden to every person who advocated this faith venture.

◆

Make a Believer
Out of Me

There are a multitude of reasons and excuses individuals give for not believing in God. Many of them, though empty are linked to many imitations in life. We question the authenticity of hair, nails, and other body parts. Jewelry, food, marriages and even our relationship with Christ are scrutinized due to the vastness of simulations in our world. Proof of authenticity therefore becomes a requisite for many who seek to evade trickery and misdirection.

As the world has its share of counterfeits, so does the house of God. Members of the body of Jesus Christ are not always immune to sly boots, a snake in the grass, or the wolf in sheep's clothing. Many individuals have been misled by false leadership and calculated behaviors intended to thwart the plan of God. To the amazement of many, Christians, like the unsaved, can misjudge character and behavior. How is this so? Many of God's children resist the counsel of the indwelling Holy Spirit. He gives us signs and warnings, but we do not always acknowledge and obey them. Instead many of us choose to believe the superficial. Existing among us is a preferred and seemingly popular reliance on behaviors that appear harmless, yet are deceitful, *"... For the Lord sees not as man sees; for man looks on the outward appearance, but the Lord looks on the heart,"* I Samuel 16:7.

The Lord tells us *"For although they hold a form of piety, they deny and reject and are strangers to the power of it; their conduct belies the genuiness of their profession. Avoid all such people, turn away from them. Wicked men and imposters will go on from bad to worse, deceiving and leading astray others and being deceived and led astray themselves,"* II Timothy 3:5–7, 13. He thus advises believers of the Lord Jesus Christ not to put faith in every spirit, but test spirits to discover whether they proceed from God because many false prophets have gone forth into the world, I John 4:1–6. In failing to listen to and obey God's voice, fractions of God's people are beguiled by the father of deception.

Indeed there are grounds for suspicion and doubt, for perpetrators and great pretenders have left horrific scars on the saved as well as the unsaved. Confusion and divisiveness are a result of their destructive works as well as preaching and teaching that negates God's plan of salvation.

The effects of insincere pious acts are considerable, for they prevent many individuals from recognizing and worshipping the Truth. Form and fashion are leading deceptive devices used by the devil to delude mankind. His strategies and choice of conduits are multiple. Through them he capitalizes on behaviors such as:

- Church attendance and membership,
- Self righteousness,
- Good Samaritanism and philanthropy,
- Busyness in church and community organizations,
- Frequent use of religious jargon,
- Religious paraphernalia,
- Scripture quoting and
- Dress codes induced by a culture or subculture.

Now all of these reactions should work to glorify God and identify a child of God, but the father of lies, Satan, has perverted many things relative to God's plan; marriage, family, sex, friendship, to name a few. Even faith has been twisted and misapplied. Because the Lord has required us to have faith in Him, many religions use faith in anything but Christ, as a requisite to deceive many unanchored and desperate individuals. Faith in anything, but Christ Jesus is a waste of time and energy. Faith in Jesus Christ is profitable and without it we can not please Him, Hebrews 11:6.

Godliness is under spiritual attack. The thief, Satan, desires to kill, steal, and destroy it in every believer's life. Why else would he work so fervently to simulate it? Yet, Christ has instructed His followers that we can do all things through Him which strengthens us. Living godly undoubtedly strengthens us. It is also a commitment to the Holy One who we have entrusted our lives. Our love and devotion towards God actually demonstrate His power and glory. He will use us in ways that are unimaginable and purposeful.

Living out the conviction to be God's man, woman, boy or girl may not always prevent the misinterpretation of godliness, but the obedient servant will bear godly fruit which evidences the presence of the Holy Spirit.

Behaving in a manner pleasing to God leads to a power filled life; a life which represents commitment to God. Such power enables us to live right before God, mankind, and spiritual wickedness. Through His righteousness alone, we are able to testify of Him, serve, worship and praise Him. In addition, we are qualified to love, forgive, and live continually for Him in the midst of opposition and travail.

As our private and public lives find favor with the Righteous God, others are drawn to Him rather than someone or something else. Such power and holiness is unlike nothing else. This, Satan can not imitate. Thus he works diligently to seduce and deceive through outward means and behaviors that even the unbelieving can perform.

Anyone with the abilities and willingness can fashion their behaviors to be a choir member, usher, or dancing and shouting church member. Such individuals can devise whatever form of behavior is expected and accepted by unsuspecting persons. However, something godly happens to us when our focus of worship, love and loyalty is to the God Who Saves. Forms of godliness actually refuse to give God His due praise and worship. To deny Him in this manner is to also be a foreigner of His divine power.

God says that we shall know them by their fruit. He later tells us what the fruit of the Spirit is. When in doubt, look for continuity and consistency in godliness. Forms of godliness and play-acting are of the flesh; therefore, they can not maintain the appearance of holiness. The divine ability to be godly endures regardless of circumstances but, forms of godliness eventually reveal one's true intentions. Herein God is glorified through His Word as He instructs us to resist haste in the laying on of hands, I Timothy 5:22.

Knowing a child of God from an imposter is difficult unless the Spirit of God usurps control in the believer's life. It is the Spirit of God who reveals the things of the Spirit. Case in point, Christ asked his disciples, *"Who do men say the Son of Man is?"* Their response was that some said that He was John the Baptist; others said Elijah; and others Jeremiah or one of the prophets. But when He asked them who did they say he was, Simon Peter answered and said, *"You are the Christ, the Son of the Living God."* Jesus responded, *"Blessed are you Simon-Bar-Jonah. For flesh and blood have not revealed this to you, but My Father Who is in heaven,"* Mark 8:27–29. Herein, we see an example where the things of God are revealed by God. Later the Spirit of God reinforces this edict in I Corinthians 2:9–15. God reveals unto us things that we can not possibly know, see, or understand. It is His Spirit that enables us to compare spiritual things with spiritual. However, the natural man, who is out of fellowship with Jesus Christ, can not appreciate the gifts, teachings, and revelations of the Spirit of God because they are spiritually discerned.

There comes a time when we all should believe in someone. Someone who is beyond reproach and perfect in every way; not a parent, sibling, spouse, child, church member, or friend. They too, need that perfect someone who knows no sin to dwell in and alter their lives. That person is Jesus Christ.

We need to align ourselves with Christ, regardless of all of the opposing acts we have seen, heard, and imagined. To believe in the Son of God is truly an act of faith; one that results in eternal security and spiritual authority.

God is real; true godliness comes from Him. It is He who is faithful, dependable, and trustworthy. We do not have to be pretentious with Him because He knows our every thought. He knows the way that we should go. He knew us before our parents and the world. It is He who has made us and not we ourselves. He is the One who is able to do exceeding abundantly above all that we can possibly ask or think.

Not only is God real, He is *for real.* He is the real thing. Coca Cola and other proposed icons can not equal or exceed Him. Afterall, He is the Creator. Without Him there would be nothing. Pretentiousness, imitations, or deficiencies can not be found in Him. He is not a *wannabe* because He is the real thing. To a certain extent, it is the self in us and the forces of evil that want to be like God. In our sinful state we, like Satan, desire God's place of majesty and worship. We want to be adored, placed on a pedestal, and seen as the greatest thing since the invention of bubble gum. Yet in the flesh, we do not want to be *good* and *holy* for His sake. That ability and desire is not in our nature, for we were born in-to sin.

God says:

"That for just as one man's disobedience the many were constituted sinners, so by one Man's obedience the many will be constituted righteous," Romans 5:19.

"As it is written, None is righteous, just, and truthful and upright and conscientious, no, not one," Romans 3:10.

"Since all have sinned and are falling short of the honor and glory which God bestows and receives," Romans 3:23.

Certainly, of our own, we do not possess the supernatural ability to be *holy*. Only God is holy. It is not in our nature to be *good* and *holy* according to God's standard of *goodness* and *holiness*. Yet, when the spirit of man or woman accepts the love of God, all things become possible.

For many, fear, confusion, rebellion and logic are dominant vices. But our faith in the God Who Saves can supersede and surpass all of these godless forces. Even the incredulous spirit can be silenced in His presence. It is through trusting and believing in the One Real God that we see who we really are and who we are purposed to be.

The saying, "I'll believe it when I see it," keeps many from knowing the Only True God. Events in the world have hardened many hearts and developed skeptical and cynical perspectives on life. Therefore, believing in someone is improbable, especially when He is invisible. The works of God are visible and sustaining. To believe that a big bang or anything other than someone with fierce and unmatched intelligence created the earth, the things on and beyond it, is truly the absurd.

7

Warped perceptions as well as real conceptions of humanity should not be allowed to hinder meeting Jesus Christ. All attempts to be good or glorify goodness without Him is wanting and void. Mere imitations of God's attributes only serve to validate that He is Lord, the Beginning and the End. Furthermore, the enemies of God substantiate His supremacy by working vigorously to nullify His works and teachings, particularly His plan of salvation. Promoting disbelief in the Lord is hard work. According to logic, it should become apparent to the unbeliever that God is an intimidating presence to the forces of darkness.

We are the very work of God, for we are fearfully and wonderfully made; the formation of our bodies and our birth is an awesome wonder, Psalm 139:13–17. Look around, desire to have your eyes opened. As Jesus said to His disciple Thomas, *"Do not be faithless and incredulous, but stop your unbelief and believe,"* John 20:27.

Seek to know the *One Real God*. Believe now and continually on Him, for it is He who pretentiousness, false humility, and form and fashion despise and attempt to masquerade as. Believe in the Omnibenevolent God who the world hates, yet endeavors to imitate solely to deceive the minds of men, women, boys, and girls. Believe in the life and purpose of Jesus Christ. He will make a believer out of you.

◆

I Think
Therefore I Am

◆

"*But whatever comes out of the mouth comes from the heart, and this is what makes a man unclean and defiles [him]. For as he thinks in his heart, so is he. Let this same attitude and purpose and [humble] mind be in you which was in Christ Jesus: [Let Him be your example in humility:]. For it is written, You shall be holy, for I am holy.*" Matthew 15:18, Proverbs 23:7a, Philippians 2:5, and I Peter 1:16.

The Lord's charge to be holy is undeniably one of the most misunderstood of His commandments. Both members of the saved and unsaved community have innocently and intentionally generated religious bigotry and confusion concerning this godly attribute. As a consequence, many people have been misled to accept tenets that are separate from the Holy Spirit's pedagogy. God is neither the author of narrow-mindedness or disorderliness. It is His will that we are clear on His expectations for us. He also expects us to live obediently to His will. Living with such purpose and conviction ultimately makes holiness an obvious feature of our persona.

Holiness begins with a mind-set or an attitude adjustment that is fashioned only by the Pure and Holy One. It is born out of a determined desire to know and do what is considered right in the mind of God. God the Father instructs us to allow the same mind and attitude of Jesus Christ to be in each of us, Philippians 2:5. We are also directed by Him to think on what is pure, Philippians 4:7. Unapologetically He issues a command to be holy, in conversation and all manner of living because He is holy, I Peter 1:15–16. Although these expectancies appear demanding and difficult, the Lord has provided His Holy Spirit to help us attain them on a daily basis. And when we fail and sin, as we will, He has put in place grace and forgiveness to return us to His righteous course: *"If we [freely] admit that we have sinned and confess our sins, He is faithful and just (true to His own nature and promises) and will forgive our sins [dismiss our lawlessness] and [continuously] cleanse us from all unrighteousness [everything not in conformity to His will in purpose, thought, and action],"* I John 1:9.

With all of our God given abilities, we are unable to manufacture holiness. It is incomparable as is its Creator. Acquisition of it through human efforts is fruitless because holiness is supernaturally given by the Holy One. For those who abide in God and permit His word to abide in them, holiness becomes a part of their testimonies. Our God exists in holiness and requires us to live accordingly. It is in this state that we truly become doers of God's word. Simultaneously, we evidence a submissive will to God the Father and rejection of earthly conformance.

Prior to our outward show of holiness, there is an inner transformation that must occur; the renewing of our mind. This intellectual conversion must eliminate the negative and accentuate the positive. The manner in which we view God, ourselves, and the world must be altered to please God and equip us for Christian service. Hence, our mode of thinking is fashioned to His liking and His perspective becomes ours. A willing attitude is everything, for how we choose to think on anything will reveal how far we acknowledge and trust God in all things.

With the power and purpose of holiness given to us, it is inexcusable for people of God to continue living submissively to our desires and the world's expectations rather than God's. Most of our desires and expectations emerge from carnal thinking and seek justification for ungodly behavior. *"Live as children of obedience to God; do not conform yourselves to the evil desires that governed you in your former ignorance when you did not know the requirements of the Gospel. But as the One Who has called you is holy, you yourselves also be holy in all your conduct and manner of living. For it is written, You shall be holy, for I am holy,"* I Peter 1:14–16.

There are three popular buttresses used as a defense for unrighteous actions: "The devil made me do it," "It's your fault," and "It just happened." We can put the blame on impulsiveness or something else, but the ability to draw a conclusion or formulate an opinion and eventually act on it lies within us. Incidentally, each of us must give an account to the Lord for all of our decisions and actions. Whether minimal or considerable time was given to develop our plan of action, we are accountable to God. He desires that we seek Him in every way. When we seek and receive the guidance of the Holy One, our obedient act becomes holy because He is holy.

Our choice of thoughts not only affect us, but our relationship with God. When we choose to think on things that are impure, our flesh aggressively nurtures those impure images so that they become our reality. We can not be committed to both pure and impure thoughts. We will esteem one over the other since where our treasure is there will our heart be also, Matthew 6:21. Whatever is in our heart will reveal itself, whether it is in a verbal or behavioral expression. Certainly the heart that is devoted to God will work to carry out the Master's plan and divorce itself from the effects of impure thoughts.

Our tainted thoughts do not produce holy conversations or actions, for the Lord tells us that executing our own impure thoughts can lead to murder, adultery, sexual vice, theft, false witnessing, slander, irreverent speech among other things, Matthew 15:19. Only when we move beyond the hearing stage of God's message and become doers of it, do we understand the deceptions found in the reasonings of self, surroundings, and Satan. *"But be doers of the Word [obey the message], and not merely listeners to it, betraying yourselves [into deception by reasoning contrary to the Truth],"* James 1:22.

There are some who share the sentiment that we are what we eat. Similarly, what we do and say is indicative of our thinking. Individuals possessing a pessimistic attitude usually lack faith that believes the impossibilities found in Christ Jesus. Attitude is everything. Therefore, it is essential that disciples of the Living God continually elect to ignore and replace impure perceptions with God's point of view: *"For God has not called us to impurity but to consecration [to dedicate ourselves to the most thorough purity],"* I Thessalonians 4:7.

Living holy is a continuous and conscious effort. Without the leading of the Holy Spirit disciples of Jesus Christ can not fulfill God's mandate to be holy. Like God's Son, we must have the Father's will as our objective. With Jesus as our model, we too can surrender every aspect of life to the Father and aim to please Him. Only in complete surrender of every area of life do we obtain holiness and purity which is acceptable to God. He wants our perspective on such concerns as relationships, professions, ambitions, health, sex, and eternity to be equivalent to His. Clarity of God's perspectives, on any issue, will bring perfect peace and divine direction in our life.

Whether through the bible, a dream, a still small voice, Christians, or other modes of communication, God does transmit His thoughts to us. We must desire to desert localized thinking and adopt His mind-set that frees us from shame, guilt, pain, and much more. Only through this mental adoption do we experience the power of holy living.

solomon

So many people equate holiness with the perfection found only in Jesus Christ. Little wonder so many people remain unsettled about becoming a Christian. What is amazing, however, is that they have enough insight to know that they can not be perfect, but not enough foresight to believe that through Him who is perfect they can be victorious in every area of their lives. Still, so many Christians are discouraged because they forget that they are not Jesus and will miss the mark from time to time. We are totally human. While on earth Christ was both human and divine. We are called to model after Him, not to be Him.

Perfection for Christians is the acquisition of spiritual maturity. As our God continually calls us to perfection, He is also telling us what is necessary for perfection. He wants us to be undivided in our loyalty and devotion to Him; unreserved in Christian service; and sincere in our relationships. We are called to be whole and complete individuals. What does this calling mean? Well, we will have scars and possibly some type of lifelong reminder of a once all consuming injury. Yet, God has healed that area of our life, because with God we can get over anything. He cleanses and closes emotional, physical and spiritual wounds. In doing so He gives the believer an additional testimony; one that is a weapon against any foe and strength for the weary. The scar or the continued reminder of an injury works to remind us of God's goodness and power. Additionally, God uses the experience of those wounded moments to employ us for further kingdom building. Every time we reflect on our harsh and injurious times we see God's mercy at work in our lives.

When we think about the very process that He decided to use to heal us, we can not help but praise His mighty work. As we think, we become. The rate of growth may vary from saint to saint, but with fortitude we will all reach the mark that pleases God. Thinking on the acts of God induce praise, witnessing, love, divine worship, and service. Herein, we realize that we are growing in the spirit and as we continue to grow spiritually, we become the perfect and unblemished people that God is looking for.

When His praises continually flow from our lips we become true worshippers of the Living God. When we think of His mercy and grace, we can not help but declare His name to all. Announcing the name of the Lord with continuance and fervor brings us to completeness. *"Whatever is true, whatever is worthy of reverence and is honorable and seemly, whatever is just, whatever is pure, whatever is lovely and lovable, whatever is kind and winsome and gracious, if there is any virtue and excellence, if there is anything worthy of praise, think on and weigh and take account of these things [fix your minds on them],"* Philippians 4:8.

Now for the skeptics who declare that certain standards for holiness are not in the bible and for the critics who judge according to personal ideals, the Lord will use any willing heart. Since the Holy Spirit knows the heart of every person, He knows who to use and what tasks to assign them to. God does not select individuals based on the premises of men and women. Usually cynical remarks against holiness are said to justify the speakers' irresponsible behavior and silence the believer. Nonetheless, those who walk and talk with God are continually instructed by Him. And for what it is worth, if the Creator thinks that someone is worthy of salvation and is useful in His Kingdom, it really does not matter what fellow creatures have to say about it.

A submissive mind-set to God evidences habitual holy thinking. Such a pattern comes from constant communion with the Lord. He is sought out in conversations and experiences throughout the day. This mode of thinking reflects a person who is at peace with God, oneself, and/or a situation. Such an individual does not allow troubles, circumstances, people, or anything other than God to dominate his/her thoughts because the Lord is above all things. Discomfort in our surroundings may remain, but keeping our mind on God evidences our trust in Him. He faithfully honors our commitment of trust in Him by giving us perfect peace, Isaiah 26:3. What a woman thinks in her heart, so is she. Yes, if we continue to think on our trials and tribulations then we become troubled. If we decide to think on God in the midst of our testing and temptations, we become content. Thinking in accordance to God's guidelines may not transpose our situation, but our relationship with Him will be strengthened and knowledge of Him increased.

It is what goes on within us that brings us to the point of wholeness with God. It is not the fashioning of the exterior, it is the constructing of the interior. So, as a man thinks in his heart, so is he. Any child of God can live holy. It is a matter of choice. Will we choose to think in conformance with the world or in the transformation given by God? There is a spiritual that says, Oh, I know I've been changed, the angels in heaven done signed my name. Christians are changed people and are expected of God to evidence our rebirth through a holy lifestyle. This is not impossible once our attitude parallels that of Christ's. What we committed to mind prior to our regeneration is reordered by the Holy Spirit. He tells us what is a priority and how to consider every thought. When we follow the directives of the Holy Spirit, we become the holy people that God the Father finds favor in.

Take my mind Holy Spirit and reorder my thoughts.

Teach me how to think on what you have done and are doing for me.

Remove anything in me that will inhibit me from giving you thanks and praise for your presence and performance in my life.

I love you Lord.

Prepare me to be a sanctuary, pure and holy, tried and true.

With thanksgiving I'll be a living sanctuary just for you.

Amen.

Who Do You
Say I Am?

A disheartening aspect of our time is the overwhelming desire to tear down the reputation and character of others. The willingness of social critics to ·give destructive criticism rather than the converse has dismantled families, disintegrated careers, and destroyed lives. Because constructive criticism is unpopular and difficult to execute, many individuals shoot the dozens, entertain rumors, read tell-all literature, and addictively give attention to gossip programming. Character assassination of people in high profile positions is not only par for the course, but a delight for those having oppositional stances. One never really knows where the criticism will come from, for relatives, associates, and adversaries are sought out to taint images of respect and honor.

Those of us who strive to live holy are under even greater attack. Like the unredeemed there will be those who delight in validating that "we are not all that." Certainly we are not all that we appear to be; therefore, it is imperative that Children Of God know what the Lord says about us. Knowing and living in this knowledge helps us when our character is under attack as well as coming to grips with our spiritual and natural selves. Whether the report of the adversary contains some truth or is totally fabricated, the Holy Spirit is ever ready to remind us of who we really are. As new creatures in Christ we are responsible for living up to God's standards and His alone. If it is not settled in our spirits that we are sinners saved by the grace of God, then we are prime targets for those who dare to use unsettled and old issues as weapons against us.

Confronting and challenging ourselves can be discomforting and a real eye opening experience. An honest evaluation will show us that we are not all that we or others think we are because of sin. But there is someone who deals with sin thoroughly. He tells us that He is the way, the truth and the life: no man can come to the Father except through Him, John 14:6. One of His specialties is image building, an unfulfilled promise of many seminars and workshops. If anyone believes and remains in Him, he makes us into the image that He is proud of, *"Therefore if any person is [ingrafted] in Christ (the Messiah) he is a new creation (a new creature altogether); the old [previous moral and spiritual condition] has passed away. Behold, the fresh and new has come!"* II Corinthians 5:17. *"And I am convinced and sure of this very thing, that He who began a good work in you will continue until the day of Jesus Christ [right up to the time of His return], developing [that good work] and perfecting and bringing it to full completion in you,"* Philippians 1:6.

We should evaluate ourselves by asking, Who am I? On the other hand we ought to consistently ask the one who matters, Who do you say that I am? His response will not be business like, churchy, or pretentious. In a way that only the Holy Spirit can execute, the truth will be revealed. Our version of self righteousness and goodness will be corrected. He tells us that our righteousness is like that of a filthy rag, Isaiah 64:6 and that we all have sinned before Him, Romans 3:23.

When I accepted Jesus Christ as my Savior and Lord, there was a reechoing of this statement from acquaintances, "You were always nice Stephannie. You do not need the church." Some individuals shared the view that my life was totally together. This misperception of me was at one time my own. However, the Holy Spirit showed me that what others thought of me was not equivalent to His perception of me. The good that others and I saw in me did not qualify me for entrance into heaven.

This word "good" is overworked and misused. Goodness in and of itself does not get us into heaven. Our actions towards others may be noble, but if our heart has not been opened to receive Christ, then our goodness is worthless in God's sight. It is a self-righteous attitude and an unsound perception of good works that will keep many a soul from reigning with Jesus. Many of these souls believe that they do not need Christ because their good works establish them as "good" people. These persons honor the laws of the land and a select group of divine directions, preferably the Ten Commandments. In so doing, they believe that they are

Changed by the Unchangeable God

One of the many lessons that the Lord teaches us is that circumstances are not supposed to have power over the child of God. Jesus agonized over the events to succeed his prayer at Gethsemane and even requested that God the Father remove them. But God did not change His mind or abort His divine plan of salvation for mankind. Our Heavenly Father can change any circumstance, but if He changed every unfortunate circumstance, we would not know the depth of His power. I have learned that as awesome as it is to experience divine deliverances in my life, the power of God is validated and authenticated when He changes the life of an individual.

We do not have the ability to change others. Subsequently, neither do we possess the supernatural ability to convert a wicked heart to one that is unbound and undefiled. Divine change in an individual emerges when the human heart willingly responds to the call of Christ. No one can call the human heart to righteous living but Christ.

God has given us freedom to choose, yet we are unable to change ourselves into the image that God appreciates and favors. Current jargon of self-help materials, as well as the ideology of self proclaimed motivational experts, is familiar to us all. I agree that we have the ability to choose some directions in our lives. In doing so, we may become successful, as success is defined personally. But what we must understand is that if what we do is not in the will of God for us, we are not successful. We may feel mature having the control to go here and there, and the very thought of someone telling us what to do and how to do it may induce anger and a sense of subservience. But we are the best that we can ever be when we are following the will of God for our lives.

God's will for us will have us living in a way contrary to the intent of the world. Only a heart changed and controlled by the Holy Spirit can withstand the persistent encounters of human and spiritual opposition in this world. The supernatural ability to persevere in spite of adversity while performing godly tasks for Christ, is not allied with our sufficiency, but is from Christ Jesus, *"Not that we are fit (qualified and sufficient in ability) of ourselves to form personal judgements or to claim or count anything as coming from us, but our power and ability and sufficiency are from God,"* II Corinthians 3:5.

We are changed by Him to execute godly tasks. Left to our own reasoning, our version of good and godly works would give glory to some god, but not the True and Living God. For this reason the Holy Spirit abides within us to ensure true and godly change. Being changed into the image of Christ is a process. The word of God identifies it as sanctification. When the process of purification begins in an area of our life, we will know it and others will too. Early in my faith walk I became discomforted when several individuals spoke of me as a changed person. Their voice tone and body language suggested that I had done something harmful to myself and disgraceful to them. I later realized that my choice to follow Christ was a threat to them, but honor for me. I thank God for giving me the opportunity to choose Him again, and again, and again.

The decision to obey God's call for holy living may cause friends and relatives to reject, ostracize, despise, and abandon children of God. And for many of God's children the fear of losing them may be overwhelming. But I have learned that what is necessary and is for our good, God allows to happen. As heartrending as it may seem, we can through Christ, do without individuals who do not bring godly purpose to our life. With God His will shall be done in earth as it is in heaven, regardless of who is willing or unwilling to get with His program. This is applicable to friendships as well as biological, marital, and adversarial relations. No one can do what Jesus does for us. Human love does not compare to the love of Jesus Christ. As much as our society values a mother's love, which in its proper perspective is valuable, it can not call life into existence, ordain a life to greatness, and save a soul from condemnation. Moreover, mother love is incapable of altering God's plan for His gift to her, the child.

God does not change, *"For I am the Lord, I do not change; that is why you, O sons of Jacob, are not consumed,"* Malachi 3:6. *"Jesus Christ (the Messiah) is [always] the same, yesterday, today, [yes] and forever (to the ages),"* Hebrews 13:8. Our unchangeable Heavenly Father will not change His plan because we or others refuse to be changed. He is sovereign and is our Creator. Who are we to advise Him on the way things ought to be? It is He who knew us from the beginning and orchestrated our lives into His majestic plan.

Although change is often difficult, we can accept God's way for living even when the change is only in us. For some of us our circumstances will not change until we do. In Job's declaration, *"... all the days of my warfare and service I will wait, till my change and release shall come,"* Job 14:14, I am reminded that in waiting for change our unchanging God is working on and for us. He is larger than our circumstance and knows how to release us from any form of affliction. Until then, He uses the process of waiting to change us to His liking.

This divine method enables us to live changed lives in the midst of torment. For some of us the release from our afflictive circumstance will come while we reside on earth. And there are others who will find relief from them when they leave earth, to be present with the Lord. Regardless of the release time, the Author and Finisher of our faith has a healing hand, and an arsenal of divine weapons guaranteed to sustain and empower us. He even uses the unchangeable circumstance to work for our good and His purpose, Romans 8:28. Someone may have intended that evil prevail in an offense towards us, but God takes what is evil and works it towards our betterment, Genesis 50:20 He is faithful in perfecting that which concerns us, *"The Lord will perfect that which concerns me; ...,"* Psalm 138:8. It is not a mystery to God of our appointed time of release, but until His revealing, appointments for blessings as well as God's choice methods of deliverance are secret to us.

Being engulfed by a circumstance is not Christ's meaning of abundant life. Bound to anything other than Him is living in opposition to His will for us. More than anything He wants to work on our heart, for our heart is more important to Him than our circumstance. Christ did not love circumstances so much that He laid down His life for them; *"God so loved the world that He gave His only begotten Son,"* John 3:16.

Christ does not change his compassions; they do not fail. He is faithful and has no respect of persons, Romans 2:11. Although our Lord uses circumstances to carry out His purposes, He does use people, particularly those born again. He promised to give those who receive Him abundant life, John 10:10 as well as a fresh start, II Corinthians 5:17. He loves us with an everlasting love. There is nothing, absolutely nothing too hard for God to resolve, Genesis 18:14 and Luke 1:37. He can change any of our concerns at the blink of an eye, but circumstances are not an issue with Him; having Christ change us is.

God in His omnipotence can allow circumstances to remain in our lives while making us new creatures in Him.

This act evidences that He is more concerned about us than unfortunate aspects of our lives. We can live a blessed life regardless of what we have been through. God may not erase bitter memories or alter history, but He can enable us to live victoriously in the present and the future. Moreover, He uses the past to help establish us in the present and the future. Entrusting our lives to Him assures us of an end that is superior to our beginning.

People are fickle, ideologies of the world whimsical, and the devil and his cohorts are running to and fro, but God, our High Tower, is constant.

Power that Pleases

Various civilizations, past and present, have placed premiums upon such things as hair, bodies, lawns, houses, animals, land, cars, gems, metals and vocations. Often the acquisition of these objects of affection is motivated out of one's desire for attention and power. Just as some of us seek to acquire these outer possessions, there must be just as much fervor placed in maintaining them. Cutting the grass and manicuring the lawn is not a one time event. With rain and sunshine the grass continues to grow. Our once clean cars are subjected to the pollutants of the air and our bodies grow in directions that we strongly desire to curtail or alter. Even relationships with our spouses, children, and friends need continual nurturing and stimulation to prevent deterioration.

If what chaos theorists believe is true, that everything is moving towards disorder and change and that there is always some form of activity working against that which we choose to preserve, then it is understandable why so many of us try to sustain "things" that we value. However, the investment of time and energy of anything that God has given to us has a place in our lives. As we strive to adduce evidence of our self-worth in the exterior person, we ought to place a high premium on the reconstruction and maintenance of the inner person. There is only one who can show us the inverse of myopic perceptions of life and direct us towards a life that is rightly established and confirmed. He is the Omnipotent God our Father who empowers those who believe in Him. Indeed this power supersedes the value placed on things of this world.

There is artistry in each of us. In Ephesians 2:10 God says, *"For we are God's own handiwork, recreated in Christ Jesus, born a-new, that we may do those good works which God predestined for us [taking paths which He prepared ahead of time], that we should walk in them living the good life which He prearranged and made ready for us to live."* We are created to do great and marvelous things for the Lord. Whether we are considered ordinary or extraordinary, God desires to use each of us for extraordinary tasks. Our Lord has enabled us, through His Holy Spirit, to do what is impossible through the flesh and oftentimes unimaginable and reprehensible to the world. Our concept of power does not compare with the power that God has given to those who believe in His Son.

So many people want the resources to live empowered lives. A buzz word of our times, empowerment has found its way into communities, families, schools, economics, professions, and churches. Many Christians are utilizing this word in conjunction with spirituality. These persons often speak of being filled with the Spirit or desiring to be like someone who appears to be spiritually together. The Lord has given every recipient of His Spirit the arsenal necessary for spiritual empowerment or holy living, *"But to as many did receive and welcome Him, He gave the authority (power, privilege, right) to become the children of God, that is, to those who believe in (adhere to, trust in, and rely on) His name,"* John 1:12.

Why then are some Christians still asking for power? Could it be that there is illiteracy to the divine tools supplied for powerful living? Is there a hindrance in the form of person, sin, circumstance, desire, or spirit that is preventing so many saints from applying the power within? Possibly some believers have not come to terms with the fact that it is God's power at work in us, which is pleasing to Him, rather than our limited descriptions of self-empowerment.

As a child of the King we have been majestically positioned to serve in a Kingdom with riches told and untold. Therefore, we must stand on what we know to be true about God and trust Him for everything. When our knowledge is limited and misguided, we can ask the Omniscient God for knowledge, wisdom, and understanding. Yes, asking our Heavenly Father a question is biblical; His word assures us of this—John 15:7, John 16:24, Matthew 7:7–11, James 4:3, I John 5:14–15, Ephesians 3:20, and Jeremiah 33:3. The divine process of asking and receiving in Jesus' name is one of God's modes of showing us that self reliance and worldly resources are impotent in comparison to Him.

God has purposefully provided believers in Christ Jesus all the essentials for this trek of faith, Philippians 4:19; however, we must be willing to accept His way for living. In obeying God's mandates we demonstrate responsibility and accountability to God, ourselves and others. This act is childlike, yet so mature.

Young children enjoy the attention of loving parents. Usually they do what it takes to acquire more attention and approval from them. The result of a parent's approval is a child who is "willing" to please. Like a child, we too must be "willing" to please our Heavenly Father who has affirmed us. Living to please God is living an empowered life. Living so comes from a heart willed to God. A heart willed to Christ is open for improvement and holy instruction. Through such acts of submission and humility, our God molds character and multiplies testimonies. It is through character building and testimony expansion that we see that the power given to us is not for our glory or for others to simply marvel over, but rather to glorify and please our Heavenly Father.

Seeing the process of empowerment at work in our lives should move us to work to maintain a favorable relationship with the Lord. Yes, I did say that we have to work. Paul tells us to continue to work out our salvation, Philippians 2:12. As able ministers of the new testament, we are expected to cooperate with God in His process that will ultimately bring out the best in us.

Continually we must open our minds and hearts for what God has for us to learn. Since everyday is unlike another, there are times that we are required to be still and observe God's work. Hearing and following His instructions are vehicles to empowerment. We don't always have to be on the move, for there are times in our walk of faith that we need to refrain from certain activities. Others may not understand our divinely led withdrawal or absence, but our faith ought to always stand in the power of God rather than the wisdom of people, I Corinthians 2:5. This act of obedience makes us teachable and open for fresh insights from our Heavenly Master. Spiritually empowered persons know who their power comes from and are wise enough to spend time with Him to get rejuvenated for the wonders that each day brings. Without acting on these requisites, we can not expect good success in the service of the Lord.

Home improvement, career development, economic empowerment at various points in life are necessary. They, like other personal choices which make our lives more comfortable, do have their place. What many persons fail to conceive is that nothing, other than God, should consume all or most of the time that God gives to us. Even our very thoughts should be monitored for prioritization, for it is God who is the First and the Last, Revelation 1:11. And it is He who we are to love with all of our heart, soul, and might, Deuteronomy 6:5. It is His Kingdom that we are to seek prior to anything else in life, Matthew 6:33. First place is reserved for God and God alone.

Indeed no self-enhancement medium can give us what God supplies. Whatever He gives simply stands in a category by itself. Satan and the world try to simulate God's gifts, weaponry, and purposes, but coming from them, is all-out perversion. Thus, as we work to maintain worldly acquirements, we must be mindful that we should seek to know God's will for us, *"For what will it profit a man if he gains the whole world and forfeits his life [his blessed life in the kingdom of God]? Or what would a man give as an exchange for his [blessed] life [in the kingdom of God],"* Matthew 16:26.

Incidentally, maintaining some things are not always comfortable and pleasurable. If we were to ask some supermodels, who many people can not imagine exercising, we would find that in order for them to remain the same dress size some form of physical workout is incorporated in their lifestyle. Whether the routine consist of stomach crunches, leg lifts, cycling, body sculpting, aerobics, running, swimming, or stair stepping, such physical exercises can be grueling when done for extended periods of time. Yet, the results for the body can be phenomenal.

Similarly, Christians must exercise faith in God. Effort has to be directed towards developing and preserving our spiritual endowments which are given to glorify God and edify His church. The process may spawn unimaginable struggles, fierce wrestling matches with ourselves and spiritual wickedness, and sleepless nights, but the Author and Finisher of our faith is faithful. He has promised to bring us through and that our end will not be like our beginning. Hallelujah! After being tried, we will come forth as refined gold, Job 23:10. As we endure the trial and remain in Him, we are promised good and perfect results.

From a consistent routine that encompasses prayer, praise, worship, bible study, scripture memory, stewardship, thanksgiving, witnessing, Christian fellowship and service, recipients of the Holy Spirit can expect Him to teach us how to utilize the power within.

Children of God have been given immense power. So great is the power of God within us that He assures us that *"Little children, you are of God [you belong to Him] and have [already] defeated and overcome them [the agents of the antichrist], because He who lives in you is greater (mightier) than he who is in the world,"* I John 4:4. Because of our belief in Christ Jesus, we have also been assured that we shall perform the great works of Jesus Christ.

Spiritual empowerment awaits anyone willing to do as Christ commands. The question for many of us is will we choose to give of ourselves for the cause of Christ? If the answer is yes, then we must position ourselves for greatness. The human heart that is bent on pleasing Him will be used for great work; production that requires priestly power. Personal power will fail, but power from our High Priest will flourish. This power at work in us is ultimately for His glory, gain, and good pleasure.

You Wear
It Well

G od tells us that disciples of Christ shall suffer, John 16:33 and II Timothy 3:12. From the new church member to the elder of the church; babes in Christ to church leaders, followers of the Messiah must go through hard times. We all have a cross to bear. Sufferance is just as much a part of Christian discipleship as is joy, Philipians 3:10. Although mystifying to some, suffering and struggling contribute to the abundant life declared by and found only in Christ Jesus.

A truism states that, "In each man's life a little rain must fall." A similar, yet stronger, declaration is spoken by Jesus Christ, "... *for He makes His sun rise on the wicked and on the good, and makes the rain fall upon the upright and the wrongdoers alike,*" Matthew 5:45 and "... *In this world we will have tribulation: but be of good cheer; I have overcome the world,*" John 16:33. Struggles are inevitably a part of every believers' life and can evolve from any area of our lives. The area in which we struggle is common to the body of Christ. Yet, the intensity and length of the contention contribute to the uniqueness of each believer's situation. Every struggle works to complete the divine process which defines, separates, and identifies children of God.

There are times when our sovereign God exposes types of suffering allocated to believers. We may witness our brothers and sisters in the faith contend with afflictions such as sickness, tumultuous relationships, unresolved issues, and economic impotence. Whether the burden is spiritually assigned or self-imposed, everyone suffers, I Peter 5:9.

We are not alone in our suffering and neither is the cross that we bear unique. Such thinking often keeps us from giving our concerns to God and sharing with prayer warriors. With such a prevailing truth, why then does it appear that some believers look good all of the time? They seem to have it all together; valuable material acquisitions, academic calibers, respectable vocations, and harmonious relationships with spouses, friends, and family. As some say, "They got it goin' on." Everything seems to be in their favor. They are blessed with a problem free life. Reality check! For what it is worth, appearing to have it all does not mean that one actually has all of the essentials for abundant living. Furthermore, many people are clueless to the personal wrestlings that were prerequisites for our spiritual victories and personal accomplishments. This misconception is re-echoed in the following two statements. "They are just spoiled in the Lord." "God just gives them too much." Such ludicrous statements are spoken by the demons of covetousness, envy, jealousy, and insecurity. These forces challenge God's presence and power in the life of the believer. Although they are high things that exalt themselves against the knowledge of God, they do not have the last word.

God's chosen people are not spoiled, but rather richly blessed and deeply loved. A spoiled person has an impaired disposition that reflects egoism. Usually the caretaker shares the responsibility for contributing to the development of this ungodly characteristic. This trait is contrary to the will of our caretaker, the Heavenly Father. Our Heavenly caretaker specializes in blessing His children for spiritual development not damaging our personalities by implanting in us narcissism, self-absorption, and greed. None of these character traits give Him the glory. Whatever we get from God blesses us and glorifies Him. As followers of the Most High God we are promised good and perfect gifts. Gifts that bring responsibility to the recipient and glory to the Lord.

Myopic images of people oftentimes minimize, distort, and even negate suffering. Some Christians join the ranks of presumers that some of us are never confronted with obstacles and do not want for anything. Occasionally I have been told that endeavors come easy to me. Nothing could be further from the truth. So often I have asked God why do I have to struggle for everything, even the simplest things. Acquiring the strongest desires of my heart involved intense spiritual wrestling. Yet, during these times I learned much about the strategies and purposes of spiritual wickedness in high places. As a result of these heavy battles, God has given me my greatest and most memorable victories. It would have been easier for me to quit and conform to the expectations of my surroundings than to trust God in my pursuits and His expectations for me. I am glad that I believed the report of the Lord, rather than the report of the world and Satan. For through my struggles, Christ taught me how to serve Him and that He reigns inspite of them. Remaining in Christ and allowing His word to remain in me during my tumultuous times proved beneficial. He matured me spiritually in ways beyond my request and comprehension.

Many outsiders often see our victories as unencumbered feats. They are clueless to the intent and extent of our struggles. God's children struggle with sleepless nights and are perplexed by the effects of an emotional pendulum that swings from jubilation to depression. Few people see our fragile moments that are filled with insecurities and idiosyncrasies. Nonetheless, we persevere trusting God who knows our frame, *"For He knows our frame, He [earnestly] remembers and imprints [on His heart] that we are dust,"* Psalm 103:14 and knows our end, Philippians 1:6. He has a way of adjusting our countenance, voice, choice of words, disposition, and thinking to give Him the glory during our season of affliction. He even keeps us during the struggle. Our minds, hearts, and bodies belong to Him rather than the circumstance. Little wonder people are unaware of our vyings. Whether God chooses to place us with our burden on display or confine it to a small group of confidants, many will marvel and stand in awe as they witness what God does to, through, and for us.

Like an outfit tailored just for us, sufferance can bring out our best. The cross that we bear is personally designed. Through Christ we are able to wear affliction well whether others are able to discern that we are indeed struggling or not. Because our God is the God who preserves and restores, we do not have to look like we have gone through ten years of famine. But if God decides to take our physical health, the Holy Spirit has a way of altering our minds to the likeness of Christ Jesus.

We must confront raging storms in life, yet Christ desires that we emulate Him completely in the process. He modeled for us how to celebrate life, fight demonic opposition, and most of all, worship our Heavenly Father. We can, through Christ, wear peace, joy, patience, self-control, goodness, kindness, faithfulness, love, humility, and confidence in atmospheres that prescribe their own dress code. It is through our body language that we depict our reliance in the Anointed One.

Because of loyalty to Christ we can expect to hear Him say, *"Well done, you upright (honorable, admirable) and faithful servant! You have been faithful and trustworthy over a little; I will put you in charge of much. Enter into and share the joy (the delight, the blessedness) which your master enjoys,"* Matthew 25:21. This kind of fruit is not cultivated and dressed from form and fashion and false humility. They are not a part of God's dress code, for they are of the flesh and are temporal. Pretentiousness and other forms of godliness do not edify Christ's church since spiritual empowerment and encouragement are not their frame of reference.

The intensity of our struggles induce a range of emotions. It is in these instances that proper godly attire be worn to credit the Greatest Designer in heaven and on earth. At all times we must totally submit to the Holy Spirit. In doing so, He will select a favorable style of dress for us to wear during our season of suffering. Whatever spiritual garb God selects for us will ultimately give Him all of the glory.

Shut In for a Glorious Purpose

Members of the claustrophobic community can attest that confinement can be a harrowing experience. Thoughts of detainment and limited liberties tend to elevate stress to levels severe to the human frame. Similarly, some prisoners serving life sentences experience this form of distress. Many of them would rather receive an accelerated death sentence than live the remainder of their lives in a confined place. Iron doors, barbed wire, miniature windows, limited sunlight, and cramped quarters can prompt feelings of despair. For many souls the severity of these conditions are enough to cause phobia and even derangement.

Unlike those who are closeted by their fears and those who are shut up for crimes against society, there is yet another group living in confinement. They are not enclosed by panic and prison, but shut in by their circumstances. Such events can be shaped by societal ills, personal choices, demonic harassment, and/or God. Yes, the Lord is responsible for separating His people. Knowing our differences and His plan for each of us, He works to develop our character and prepare us for ministry in ways that boggle the human mind. Shutting us into a situation is one of His methods of preparation for the labor of love.

Although our love for God is great, He requires more from us. Greater work needs to be done and God has chosen us for the job. To ensure the kind of mind-set necessary for the tasks, our Heavenly Father locks us up and secures the key of our release until His time of fulfillment. Whether the lesson is for us or someone else, only the Lord knows when to open the door. Until then we must establish an attitude that works with God during this experience; one that seeks His perspective entirely.

Indeed, this form of readiness is necessary for divine assignments. Guarding the door of our situation and working one on one with us ensures our spiritual transformation. Such a miraculous and intentional work guarantees that we will not be the same individuals when we come out of our shut in experience.

Noah was shut in by God along with members of his family. God found favor in Noah and spared his life. Yet, through his life God used him and continues to use His witness for His glory and our growth. One can only imagine the conversations Noah had with God during his sequestration. Probably not in his wildest dreams did Noah think that God would use him in the ways actualized. This servant of God heard and obeyed God's directives for constructing an ark, preaching righteousness to the ungodly, and managing an enormous cargo. The Lord continues to use Noah's devotion centuries after his death to help ground individuals in Christ.

Chapters 6–9 of the book of Genesis clearly tell Noah's story; however, it is chapter 7 verse 16 that captures my attention—*"And they that entered, male and female of all flesh, went in as God had commanded [Noah]; AND THE LORD SHUT HIM IN AND CLOSED THE DOOR ROUND ABOUT HIM."*

It does not take a rocket scientist to comprehend the cause of the great flood. Rather than live by God's standards, the people devised and lived according to their own. God destroyed the rebellious and preserved the righteous. The Lord's favoritism towards Noah is crystal-clear, yet God saw beyond the flood. He knew that with further chiseling of Noah's character He could entrust him with greater responsibilities.

There was no way out of the ark unless the Lord made a way. Even when it appeared safe to step out on dry land, God made Noah wait until He opened the door of the ark. The closed door signified that work was still necessary and miracles were still being performed *inside* as well as outside of the ark.

No one knows what goes on behind closed doors is a familiar adage, but it is evident in this passage of scripture that God performed a major work on Noah and his family behind a shut door. Other scriptures come to mind that coincide with this kind of event. One, it was behind a shut door that the Lord used a jar of oil to fill many empty vessels for a desperate widow, II Kings 4:1–6; Elisha was used of God to revive a dead child behind a shut door, II Kings 4:8–37; and the resurrected, but not yet ascended, Christ spoke to and showed Himself to a group of fearful disciples behind closed doors. Behind those closed doors they received the Holy Spirit, John 20:19–26. Until Christ returns, the Lord will use closed doors and shut in situations as one of His many ways to perfect that which concerns us and to continue His good work in us.

Although Jonah's shut in experience varied from Noah's, he too can testify of the personal transformation that occurs when one is shut in round about. It is our spiritual transformation that ultimately gives the Lord all of the glory and all of the praise.

The bible says that every beast, every creeping thing, every bird—and whatever moves on the land—went forth by families out of the ark. Apparently not one living thing was lost during their stay in the vessel. Noah remained responsible for the things of God and opened himself for God's instruction while in a place of safety and schooling. With conveniences removed from his life, the Lord foreknew that Noah would continue to testify of Him. Once on dry ground Noah built an altar to the Lord and offered Him burnt offerings of praise and thanksgiving. Over 300 days in a confined place and still the love for God remained in Noah's heart. Noah may have wrestled with God and himself while shut in, but it was his love for God that got him a pronounced blessing.

Noah was blessed for his steadfastness and commitment. We too can be blessed by the same God who has no respect of persons. This saint triumphed over criticism, mockery, and perplexity. In his confinement he had to exercise trust in God like he had never known.

Noah found favor from God because of his faith in God. He and his family were delivered and immensely blessed. Yet, as blessed as he was Noah was not given all of the specifics of God's plan. Some things he would learn of in God's time. It is through this method of God that we find ourselves ever dependent upon Him. Not having every aspect of the blessing revealed Noah had to depend on God to direct him to the pairs of animals. Dependence, reliance, and expectancy in the Lord for continued security, food, and so much more was ever present. As much as we are blessed we still need God. Case in point, the Lord answers a prayer for the acquisition of a job, spouse, child, home, ministry, or other desire, but living with the responsibility of the blessing often is laborious. How then do we successfully handle the blessing? Only through dependence on God in the step by step and day to day process can we ever be assured of having good success in all that we do. Consequently, not knowing every detail of God's course for us should *never* keep us from doing His will. Just as Noah followed through, so should we.

We may not be confined in an ark but in God's way and time obedient children of God will experience fruit born out of a divine confinement. This kind of confinement is always for His purpose. And although we may compare it to imprisonment, with the Lord it is a vehicle to spiritual freedom and empowerment. Through the experience we become more than conquerors.

Several changes in us occur when the Lord shuts the door and closes us in. One, God works on our heart and our mind that He will have control of them. He wants total surrender from us for it is the willing heart He uses best. Absolute surrender is a process that involves an *attitudinal* change. Having the mind of Christ is one of the Lord's goals for us. This is not possible when we refuse to accept God's methodology.

Surrender to the Lord's will is evidenced when He is permitted to have His way. It really is about Him doing what He wants to do in us as long as and how He wants to. "Not my will, but yours Lord," becomes more than a declaration but a desire and a decision.

As good as we are now and as righteous as Noah was prior to the flood, we are still diamonds in the rough. God has to saw, round, lop, and polish us. This process is continual; like a diamond there are several facets to us. Only God knows when the cut is right. It is through the cutting that determines our brilliance. Thus, it is to our benefit to allow God to cut away. For at the appropriate time, we, like diamonds, will produce the greatest possible brilliance.

Diamonds do not become jewels until they have been chiseled, cleansed, and buffed. Even then cutting and polishing the rough diamond is a slow and costly process. The process must be done by highly trained workers. God likens us to jewels, Malachi 3:17. We are His handiwork. It is with great skill and patience that the Lord works on us. His goal, like the diamond cutter, is to produce a jewel that possesses power to reflect light, the Light of the World.

It is our submission to God that leads us to the jewel stage. Our heart, mind, and our very life have got to belong to Him. In addition to submission, patience is given to us during our confined season. Here we learn to exercise patience properly because we do not have much choice. It may take some of us longer than others to acquire it but we will possess it. God has shut and closed the door round about. There is no where to go. No matter how hard we try to escape or lean towards something other than Him, defeat and frustration meet us. Nothing can bring us out but God. We may speak compromise, defeat, even death, but most of us don't really want them. We want an easier process. We do want to live, just not God's way. It is through our steadfastness and patient endurance that we shall win the true life of our souls, Luke 21:19.

It is not unusual for our circumstances to worsen while we are shut in. Desperately we want to break out and fix it but there is no breaking out when God is in control of the door. Whether increased pressures are sent to take our focus off of the Lord or draw us closer to the Lord, they are not bigger than our God. *"The waters became mighty and increased greatly upon the land, and the ark went gently floating upon the surface of the waters,"* Genesis 7:18. God has a way of floating us gently above our circumstances. He does not always remove us from them but if we let Him, He will teach us how to put them under our feet. Although God has all power and can do anything, there are moments when He calls us to action. He will enable us to float *gently* on rough waters when we become tenacious and persistent in the things of God. Such willful acts demonstrate faith, trust, reliance, devotion, and commitment in the Lord.

Being the jealous God that He is, the Lord occasionally wants us to know who or what is at the forefront of our heart and mind. Have we yielded to other voices because God did not do what we wanted Him to do when we wanted it done? Did the questions and misconceptions of others sway us to abandon God's route for us? He wants what has taken His place. We should never give up on God or make Him less than our first priority. In spite of the temptations and trials in life we can prevail, for the race is not given to quitters but to those who endure to the end. *"Therefore, my beloved brethren, be firm, immovable, always abounding in the work of the Lord, always being superior, excelling, doing more than enough in the service of the Lord, knowing and being continually aware that your labor in the Lord is not futile, it is never wasted or to no purpose,"* I Corinthians 15:58. God gives us enough service to do while shut in. Because things are not going our way this is no cause to go AWOL. Satan may tell us that serving God is worthless since we are enduring such rough times, but it is continued and consistent service for Christ that works to strengthen us. He will honor our patience and steadfastness.

The Lord will not stir the same way all of the time. He may be silent but His silence does not affirm His absence. He promised to be with us even until the end of the age and never to leave or forsake us. In those moments know that He will speak. However, openness is essential if we plan to absorb what He has to say. God's silence towards the heart bent towards Him actually works to prepare and strengthen us. Although we may not see it initially, noticing that God is silent is a sign that we are in His will. For to seek God is His desire for us.

Time may seem to work against us but time is not to us what it is to the Eternal God. Time in a closed in situation can make us more dependent on Him. The length of our stay in a shut in situation may entice us to reason or rationalize a plan of our own but there is no way out, really out, until God opens the door. And there is no success in what we do because God's hand is not in it. All God has is time. The opportunistic perverter of truth will attempt to use time to discourage us and provoke us to act on our own with haste. His hope is that we will tire of the wait and operate out of the flesh, thus giving up the promise and letting go of the belief in God's message to us. Therefore, it is useful for us to work with God in these moments. Praising, serving, and worshipping Him must not cease. In so doing, we will see that being confined will not move us as the flesh, world, and ruler of darkness expected it to.

In the field of education there is a teaching strategy called "wait time." Its intent is to give every student a reasonable amount of time to respond to a given question or statement. Our Heavenly Teacher gives us wait time also. He gives us a specific time to respond to His commands and advice. What Satan does is interfere with our wait time. He causes distractions so that our focus on God and the things of God are teetered. Therefore, time to transfer, process, and reflect on God given information is fractional or shortlived.

In spite of the devil's antics, our Heavenly Father is long suffering and patient. In His classroom, if we remain, we are guaranteed spiritual growth. We may have to be retained until a lesson is learned and essential skills are acquired but promotion from the Lord will come. Time spent in His classroom will work for our good. The school of hard knocks will be used to prosper us in Him. Even when we have to repeat a lesson, He continues to teach with much love and power. Our season will come for graduation day. Whether the lesson was extended or short, time spent in class with God is never a waste.

Time alone with God forces us to see ourselves truthfully. The Lord will show us aspects of ourselves that represent self-centeredness and other vices that are not in His will for us. The flesh detests the truth so be prepared to fight; to wrestle with yourself. An uprising of the flesh will work vigorously to thwart God's will for us. Do not yield to its' maneuvers. Yield instead to the absolute control of the Holy Spirit. Regardless of how sensible it seems to do things suggested by the mind or an intelligent friend, hold on to what God has spoken into your spirit. And when it becomes necessary, talk to yourself. Encourage yourself in the Lord. Know when to admonish your moods, emotions, desires, and thoughts in Jesus' name.

Noah waited years for the promise of God to manifest.

Being flesh and blood as you and I, it interests me to know what His wait time was really like. One thing is for sure, whatever He endured during the wait for the promise, He was available and obedient to the Lord. Because of his obedience, the ark was completed by the 120th year; God's timeline for the destruction of flesh. He did not lose hope and trust in the Lord. My friend Noah remained steadfast and unmovable in his faith. He abounded in God's work; building the ark and preaching to the unbelieving of his time.

God's plan for us goes beyond what we see. Although Noah and his household were saved because of his righteousness, God saw beyond the flood. Knowing that destruction was promised, Noah could not foresee how his obedience would affect you and I. He had to be prepped for the next phase of God's plan because He would be given other divine assignments. The success of them, according to God's standards, would be predicated on his reception and obedience to God's directives. When we allow God to prepare us effectiveness and favor from God is guaranteed.

What every Christian needs to understand is that being shut in does not mean that we are shackled. Having the escape hatch or exit closed by the Lord does not signify bondage. Rather it is a loving act that can save and expose us to truths that empower and permit us to continually stand in and for Him. We are empowered by the Lord to be His witnesses. Through shut in experiences we gain fresh testimonies of what God can and will do for those who trust Him. Our testimonies will advance from the milk and elementary stages to solid food and spiritual maturity, Hebrews 5:11–14 and 6:1–6, for stagnation is not what God desires for the saints. We serve a progressive God.

Shut in experiences from the Lord culminate with God's pronouncement of our blessing. He remembers our faithfulness, submission, devotion, obedience, patience, time, steadfastness, and attitude towards Him. When we are instructed to go forth from the situation of confinement, God exposes to all what we have acquired by remaining with Him. We have more than we started out with prior to being shut in. Like Job, Noah's end surpassed his beginning. Survey the very life of Jesus Christ, the Author and Finisher of our faith. His very name conquered death and the grave. He now sits on the right hand of the throne of God. He was in a shut in situation by God but God brought Him majestically out. His obedience to the Father afforded Him more than the world or Satan could ever offer.

I am shut in for a divine purpose, ought to be our response to our divine confinement. The door will only open when the required work in us is completed by the One who permanently opens and seals. Let us work with Him as He works on us. This act of obedience will enable us to tell someone what really goes on behind closed doors.

---◆---

Life for the
Living Dead

---◆---

F rightened, confused, and desperate Tamar pleaded to
a misguided man for the preservation of her virginity
and sanity. She knew that the consequences of losing
them would severely mar both her self and societal worth.
Fearfully, Tamar considered the aftermaths for herself and
her brother Amnon. The Spirit of the Lord says in II Samuel 13:12–13, *"She replied, No, my brother! Do not force and
humble me, for no such thing should be done in Israel! Do not do this
foolhardy, scandalous thing. And I, how could I rid myself of my
shame? And you, you will be [considered] one of the stupid fools in
Israel. Now therefore, I pray you, speak to the king, for he will not
withhold me from you."*

In spite of her efforts to make Amnon understand that
no means no, her impassioned protests were rejected. Her
objections, considerations, and suggestions to a perverted
passion meant nothing to him. It is highly conceivable that
Amnon was clueless to the sequence of violence, discord,

and destruction that would frequent his family as a consequence of his egomaniacal choice and incestuous act.

Once declassed and degraded, Tamar ceased to dream. Something died within her which produced her abyss of hopelessness. Amnon had little to no regard for her life; how she would be adversely labeled by society, undesired as a wife, and denied parental bliss. Her dreams did not evolve into her reality.

As a result of this unfortunate experience, a melancholy spirit entered into the life of Tamar. So unhappy was she that the Holy Spirit says, *"So Tamar dwelt in her brother Absalom's house, a desolate woman,"* II Samuel 13:20. She was empty, ineffective, but above all, without joy. Temporal solace was found in the companionship of her brother Absolom who advised her to hold her peace and not to regard the matter because Amnon was her brother. She, like so many rape victims, was expected to disavow her pain through silence and secrecy. Such practices of denial and shame lead to a life of torment, but those who advocate honesty embrace healing.

The sexual experience with Amnon was so burdensome to Tamar, that she believed life would be extremely difficult for a king's daughter. *"And I, how could I rid myself of the shame?"* was the question that slept and walked with her. It was ever present. Limited support from family and acquaintances assisted in her decision to leave the life of leisure to that of seclusiveness.

The questions, shame, and loneliness, haunted Tamar's spirit so, that she became a woman devoid of joy. She found it extremely difficult to move beyond this experience. Even if she considered reentering the palace walls, moving on, or burying this pain, her mind would not let her. Continually she confronted the demon who told her that she could not rise above her pain or move beyond this oppressive state. She eventually embraced several spirits which contributed to her state of hopelessness: two were despondency and brokeness. A sick heart and physical deterioration soon ensued after their arrival. *"Hope deferred makes the heart sick ...,"* Proverbs 13:12 and *"..., but a broken spirit dries up the bones,"* Proverbs 17:22. As a team they worked until they secured a permanent state of depression. This beautiful woman was awake, yet dead. She breathed, yet was lifeless, for she found it easier to abandon hope than hurt.

Tamar lived, but how she lived is the account that saddens me. She perceived herself as worthless and impure. Because of the disrespect imposed on her, she chose to dwell in her brother Absolom's house as a sequestered and unproductive individual; a woman devoid of warmth and hope. I can only imagine that to live with her or even be in her presence was to feel a little of her torment because her depression was that intense.

Everyone may not identify with Tamar's insectuous experience; however, in every Christian's life a trial or tribulation comes along that strains the inner most part of our being. Rather than seeing these moments as opportunities to grow in the faith of Jesus Christ, many of us desire to succumb to resignation of the faith. Our smiles become plastic, if we have any at all, and behaviors pretentious and expected rather than Christ-controlled.

It is in moments of cheerlessness that we are instructed to be of good cheer for Jesus has overcome the world. In all appearances cheer is good, afterall it brings a smile, laughter and other pleasant feelings. But all smiles and laughter are not generated from things that are good in the eyes of the Lord. Having good cheer is the result of finding delight, satisfaction, and even courage in the things of the Lord. Such experiences continually teach us that it is through these things that we live victoriously in every circumstance. It is good cheer that reflects our joy in the Lord. Knowing that Christ has overcome, we are His, and that He lives in us is cause for unswayable joy.

The Lord's joy is unlike happiness which is a temporary state of contentment based solely on favorable outcomes or sensual joy which is the gratification of a fleshly or worldly appetite. His joy is the supernatural ability to be content in both favorable and unfavorable circumstances. It is the joy of the Lord that is our strength during tough times, not happiness. The Lord describes His joy as unspeakable, full, complete, strong, and exceeding. And once one has experienced it, it is not something that we want the Lord to ever remove. Yes, this joy the world can not give and certainly Tamar did not possess.

Perhaps Tamar thought that God could not alter her state of despair. While undesirability and dirtiness circled her spirit, she shared the thoughts of many, that when we, our situations and surroundings are unclean, fellowship with

God is difficult. The Lord has clearly informed us that, *"For with God nothing is ever impossible and no word from God shall be without power or impossible of fulfillment,"* Luke 1:37. The Lord can and is willing to reach us at any state. Disgrace and infamy are no exceptions.

In regard to a familiar maxim, cleanliness is next to godliness, physical and environmental cleanliness is not a prerequisite to knowing or doing what the Lord commands. The Lord tells us that He heard and delivered Daniel in a filthy lions' den. In a grimy dungeon the Lord accompanied and delivered Paul and Silas. In an unsanitized stable the Word of God was birthed in flesh full of grace and truth. The Lord is not intimidated by filth. He can reach the vilest heart and move in the foulest of circumstances. Many dirty people stood next to Christ to be blessed by Him over 2,000 years ago and certainly many unclean hearts and bodies are being blessed by Him today.

Grimy clothes, unwashed bodies, unsterile surroundings or impure acts should not be considered barriers that inhibit anyone from experiencing Jesus. The Lord is never too busy or removed from us that He can not hear or help us. He sees and knows everything. He even tells us that if we make our bed in hell He'll find us there, Psalm 139:8. Hence, we ought to esteem God regardless of the condition of our surroundings. Cleanliness next to godliness ought to denote that a heart bent towards God will exhibit Christlike behaviors and attitudes whether one's surroundings are tainted or untainted.

There is no doubt that the thief, the devil, came into Tamar's life to steal, kill and destroy. To remain in a state of desolation reflects her loss of so much, particularly hope and joy. The very things that the enemy sets out to take away from us he also uses to sever our relationship with God. He is always betting that through our tribulation he can terminate our trust, hope, and development in Christ Jesus. That is why when we seem overwhelmed by life's experiences we must ask the Lord for direction and understanding. He will let us know what is necessary, for whatever is necessary is for our good. On the other hand Satan will attempt to use the immensity of our trials to entomb us and denounce the power of God.

When we are spiritually bankrupt, we need a Living God who sees, understands, and remedies our dilemma. For those experiences that bring grief and hopelessness, we need the God of the Disconsolate. He is concerned with helping those who can not help themselves, for severed from Him we really are ineffective, John 15:5. Benjamin Franklin's assessment that, "God helps them that help themselves," is partially true[1]. The True and Living God is also the God of the Oppressed. He specializes in helping those who have no resources, have tried everything but Him and are too foolish to know that He is necessary.

The Lord has promised that none of us will be plucked out of his hand, John 10:29, that the flood will not overwhelm us and we shall not be burned by the fire, Isaiah 43:2. Without a doubt we are precious to Him who says that we are redeemed and belong to Him. Furthermore the Lord has promised us joy that no man can take away from us, John 16:22.

"The thief comes only in order to steal and kill and destroy: I came that they might have and enjoy life, and have it in abundance (to the full, till it overflows)," John 10:10. With Him there is no problem that can not be solved or circumstance that is beyond repair. We were not created by God to live as barren vessels. The Holy Spirit tells us that we possess precious treasure [the divine Light of the Gospel] in our earthly vessels, II Corinthians 4:7. Through Him we are not dead, but alive. We have the Holy Spirit within who quickens us. He stimulates our minds and revives our hearts. Because of Him we are creatures of joy, light, and productivity. It is not God's will that we live without these attributes, for in each we experience the purpose of Christ's convergence—that we may have abundant life.

No one, including Tamar, could rid her of the shame which led her to a desolate state. She was cold, unresponsive, lonely, cheerless, unproductive and forsaken. She breathed, but the joy of life did not dwell within her. Buried and burdened by her own despair she gave off such a spirit of gloom that her brother Absolom would later kill the perpetrator who stole her joy. Incidentally, Tamar was not responsible for neither of her brothers' choices. Sadly, their choices, as well as her own plea, *"I pray you, speak to the king, for he will not withhold me from you,"* were mere reflections of their frame of reference. As offspring of an anointed, yet wayward king, the three of them witnessed how selfish passions consume and control, II Samuel 11 and 12. Added suffering was impounded upon her family because of her father's and brothers' actions, not the Lords'. When evil begets evil and resistance to the words of Jehovah persist, there is no real remedy or healing, II Chronicles 36:16. Tamar's issues were not resolved by Absolom's invitation to his home nor his plot to murder Amnon. She remained a desolate woman in spite of these fleshly solutions.

Christ does not desire for his children to live desolate, for it is a misrepresentation of His purpose. He is *full of* life, hope, joy, truth and many other spiritual benefits. *"It is out of His fullness that we have all received [all had a share and we were all supplied with] one grace after another and spiritual blessing upon spiritual blessing and even favor upon favor and gift [heaped] upon gift,"* John 1:16. We will become depressed, discouraged, and disconcerted at times. We may even experience desolation in a relationship, ministry, or profession, but God is the God of Life and the Resurrection. He is able to give us the necessities for perseverance which give Him the glory and us a fresh testimony. He specializes in doing new things, especially in the barren areas of our life.

Coincidentally, when barrenness, an offshoot of desolation, enters our lives, it is sometimes identified as a wilderness or desert experience. Nothing seems to be growing in our lives and by all accounts our relationship with God often seems distant and stationary. Although there are similarities in these experiences, they are not identical. I perceive spiritual barrenness to be a grievous state which does not permit God to fill a specific void in our lives. The abyss exists because God has not been invited into a situation or area that needs altering which is essential for spiritual empowerment. These empty chambers of the human heart are inhibitors to spiritual development and reflect one's disenchantment towards the things of God.

Wilderness and desert experiences on the other hand appear bleak and bare, but actually are full of God's knowledge and wisdom. Regardless of what we see and do not see, God is working on our behalf. Such an experience is not devoid of His presence and power. Unlike spiritual barrenness, spiritual reproduction occurs in the wilderness and desert experiences. Yes, there is life in the wilderness and desert. Animals and people have learned to survive in such harsh regions for thousands of years because God has made a way for them to live, *"I will even make a way in the wilderness and rivers in the desert,"* Isaiah 43:19b. We are comforted by His oasises; fertile green spots in dry situations. He utilizes and leads us in these episodes of life to draw us closer to Him and to spiritually empower us. When we emerge we bear new spiritual fruit and account for productivity in the Kingdom of God. While in the desert or wilderness, Jehovah Jireh supplies every need and infuses our desires with His.

To our continual amazement the Lord does new things, particularly in desolate lives. He tells us in Isaiah 43:19a, *"Behold I am doing a new thing!"* Performing and establishing new things in our lives is God's business. He alone is an expert in doing all things well. He is able to rebuild relationships, situations, but above all he remakes us when we accept Jesus Christ as Savior and Lord. As new creatures in Christ, we are filled with the authority of God. It is this power that enables us to live victoriously and joyously through all things. It is these characteristics that reflect abundant life; life that only Jesus Christ can give.

Contrary to a pervasive belief that God will give us anything that we want, the Lord does place some conditions on us. One being, that we must believe that Jesus is who He says He is. When two blind men requested physical sight from Jesus, they acknowledged his Messianic purpose, saying, *"Have pity and mercy on us, Son of David!"* Without seeing any of his works, they knew that He was the Messiah. Jesus' question to them was *"Do you believe that I am able to do this?"* Because they knew His identity and purpose, they answered, *"Yes, Lord."* Their confidence prompted the Lord's reply, *"According to your faith and trust and reliance [on the power invested in Me] be it done to you,"* Matthew 9:27–29. Hence, their eyes were opened because they believed, without seeing, that Jesus was who He claimed to be.

When we acknowledge Jesus as Lord, we will ask in accordance to His will and thus be blessed. The Lord accentuates His Lordship in John 16:24, *"Up to this time you have not asked a [single] thing in My Name [as presenting all that I am]; but now ask and keep on asking and you will receive, so that your joy (gladness, delight) may be full and complete."* Asking in Jesus' name reflects our belief that only through and because of Him can we receive that which is essential for us.

In addition, we must believe that the Lord desires abundant life for us: *"I came that they may have and enjoy life, and have it in abundance (to the full, till it overflows),"* John 10:10.

Oftentimes people in a desolate state see themselves as unworthy of the benefits Christ offers. Self-pity, self-hatred, and self-scrutiny have severely altered perceptions of themselves and the people around them. Tamar's seclusive lifestyle bears witness to such impressions.

Such self destructive thoughts promote the belief that others, including Jesus Christ, sees one as unworthy of joy, peace, and success. To live joyously one must acknowledge that Christ is the resurrection and the life we need. He not only has the power to give eternal life, He gives life to the spiritually dead, depressed, disgarded, and disconsolate among us. Whatever the thief snatches or kills, our hope, joy, peace, warmth, courage, zeal, kindness, confidence, wit, or motivation, the Lord is able to recover and resurrect it. And whatever He establishes or reestablishes in our lives always overshadows what was snatched and snuffed away maliciously. Thus one whose spirit has been resurrected will possess and exhibit the fruit of the Holy Spirit which is a true indicator of God's holy presence, purpose, and power.

Another requisite for victory over a desolate state is to believe that through God's promises we can move beyond that seemingly point of no return. Christ told us that in this world we will have tribulations, but to be of good cheer because He overcame the world, John 16:33 and that because we are of Him we have overcome them, I John 4:4a. Undoubtedly we are overcomers. The spirits of this world, desolation and depression to list a few, are not commissioned to rule over us.

Through Christ we can do all things, Philippians 4:13. He gives us success in moving beyond desolate times. What is done is done. We can not change the past. We may be taken down by the terrors of life or have said some things that we can not retract, but God who favors no person above another has devised ways for us to be in right relation with Him, *"We must all die; we are like water spilled on the ground, which cannot be gathered up again. And God does not take away life, but devises means so that he who is banished may not be an utter outcast from Him,"* II Samuel 14:14.

The Lord wanted to know if Ezekiel believed that life and hope could reign in a valley of immense desolation. And yes Martha, Lazarus' devoted sister, was asked also by the Lord if she believed that His authority would bring life to her desolate situation. In each instance, Christ proved that desolation is impotent when He is on the case. Each of these witnesses experienced first hand desolation and divine deliverance. Because desolation is inferior to the power of God, anyone relying on the Master can move beyond and even have power in a desolate state.

Moving on does not necessarily mean being removed from a desolate situation, for the Lord does not bridle every adverse circumstance in our lives. It is us that he died for and promised to support and return for not our circumstances. He enables us to grow and develop in the midst of the fire, and the flood. Because of Him we are not burned or overwhelmed. For such we ought to thank Him continually.

Christ does not speak out of the side of his neck. He says what He means and means what He says. With His words and works as witness, we should believe that through Him we can make it, move on and live again. Even for those who are too despondent to believe, Christ's love extends beyond despondency. He affords everyone the opportunity for ample life while temporal residence is ours on earth because in his favor is life, Psalm 30:5a.

The inability to find resolve to her continual sadness has made Tamar's story one of the most grievous accounts in the bible. Some persons may be unable to relate to her pain, but there is a circumstance that has the potential to reduce each of us to the same measure of sadness that Tamar experienced or worse. Thus, it would be foolish for us to discard the potency and possibility of desolation in any area of life. Whether familiar or foreign to us, the devil is seeking to sift us as wheat. Evidence of his works—thievery, annihilation, and devastation—are everywhere. Yet, it is with the hope, love, and joy found only in Christ Jesus that I can say that desolation is not the end. We do not have to lay down and wither away.

I wish that the impact of someone's testimony and God's promise that weeping may endure for a night, but His joy comes in the morning, would have altered her outcome. Her tears and incestuous experience did not have to leave her barren and hopeless. Whatever the span of her night experience and whatever amount of time she needed to heal, God would not be short on His promise to give her joy.

Just maybe if someone would have told her that the Lord's joy would establish a personal song that even the angels can not sing, she could have lived as a prosperous woman rather than desolate one. To hear her sing it would be to know of the Lord's joy, hope, deliverance, and love. This Spirit inspired song surely would have triggered a smile, laughter, and praise in Tamar and blessed her kin. Instead her depression promoted a spirit of mournfulness that permeated the King's household.

During and after our period of heavy-heartedness the Lord is willing to establish a song in our hearts, for He is our song as well as our strength, Psalm 118:14. The Lord will do what He deems necessary to assure us that remaining downcast is not His desire for us. Through His song to us, He will confirm His Lordship and encourage us in Him. His words assure us that there is a time of rescue, relief and resurgence, *"For, behold, the winter is past; the rain is over and gone. The flowers appear on the earth; the time of the singing [of birds] has come, and the voice of the turtledove is heard in our land,"* Song of Solomon 2:11–12. We are guaranteed not just a song, but a new song which is our fresh testimony, *"O sing to the Lord a new song ...,"* Psalm 98:1.

We must commit to memory that being wounded, dejected, tempted, and even murdered, Jesus found strength, joy, and confidence in God the Father. Death, discrimination, and dejection were not His end because He is the Beginning and the End, The First and Last to whom nothing compares. He did not allow anything or anyone to separate Him from the Father's love. Christ Jesus stood above what many of us would consider desolate circumstances. As He lived so can we. He would not have told us so if we were incapable of it. The Spirit of God can raise us above every one of life's sorrows. Desolation may take us down, but it is the power and love of God that assures desolation and any demon that not only do we belong to God, we shall remain with God. I concur with Paul, *"If God be for us who or what can be against us?"*

With every temptation and affliction that confronts us, we are created to be overcomers. Despite the pain of any circumstance, it is inferior to the power of God. Molestation, abortion, rejection, abandonment, like other forms of evil can not consume us: *"It is because of the Lord's mercy and loving kindness that we are not consumed, because His [tender] compassions fail not,"* Lamentations 3:22. Neither will such things separate us from the love of God, Romans 8:35–39. It is His love that empowers us to live inspite of hurts and resurrects us when all hope appears to be gone. Like King David, we too can declare that we will not die but live, and shall declare the works and recount the illustrious acts of the Lord.

Christ promised us that through Him we can do all things. Through Him we live and are revived. Desolation, like any vice can not determine our fate, for we are ordained to be about greatness through Him who is the Life and the Resurrection. No matter how far down we go, He can find and resurrect us. Our destiny is not in the stars, cards, or on our palms. It is in the almighty hands of God; hands that no one can take us out of.

The whisper of Satan may be to curse God and die, but look to Jesus and live. The presence of evil may be over-whelming, but believe Jesus and live. I do not know how God does it, but He is able to establish and renew us. Through Him we can begin again. Satan attempts to establish our end through desolate times. His mission is to take anything away from us that gives us victory. Stealing, killing, and destroying our will to live is a priority to him. It is through these means that he perceives our end, but he is not like the All Knowing and Wise God. He can not fill the Lord's shoes. Only God knows the end of anything because He is the Beginning and the End. Nothing is over until God says that it is over. He is the Resurrection and the Life. Whoever believes in Him, although he may die, shall live. And who-ever continues to live and believe in Him shall not die at all, John 11:25–26. The Spirit of God also tells us that, *"there is a latter end [a future and a reward], and our hope and expectation shall not be cut off,"* Proverbs 23:18 and *"Better is the end of a thing than the beginning of it, and the patient in spirit is better than the proud in spirit,"* Ecclesiastes 7:8.

When our joy and song are stolen, we can regain them. We must consider that our God makes what is crooked straight and works everything in our lives out for our betterment. There is no gloom nor adverse experience that is too hard for the Lord to annihilate and overpower. Such things are under His feet becoming our footstool. He is very capable of setting a table for us in their presence. Because nothing is impossible with Him, His worshippers do not have to lay down and die without hope. We do not have to give in to the overwhelming pain of tragedy and the power of depression, despondency and desolation.

I can not say this enough, look to Jesus and live. He is able and willing to free us from the seduction of melancholy and self destructive spirits. He promises us that whoever He sets free of anything is absolutely free, *"So if the Son liberates you [makes you free men], then you are really and unquestionably free,"* John 8:36. Trusting God who is faithful to His every word will give freedom and new life to anyone. In return for our afflictions and tears, He gives us peace, power and prestige. Abundant life is what the Lord is about disbursing. Wholeness and restoration is continually his aim for His people and no situation of ours can deter God from His ultimate purpose for us. Until the Holy Spirit gives us vision, understanding, and desire, our eyes can not conceive, ears are unable to comprehend, and hearts without reception to what God has purposed for us. He has reserved notable tasks and superior blessings for those who worship Him in spirit and in truth. Without His leadership, we are clueless to our purpose and the direction He desires for us.

I believe that God wants to use us and our experiences to glorify Him. There is a time under heaven for everything and for many Christians the time is now to be discharged from the restraints of wickedness and to prosper in the realm that God has ordained for them. Indeed spiritual emancipation is at hand and God is our freedom fighter. His cause becomes clear when we desire to be disburdened from what is consuming us. He becomes an all consuming fire to us the moment we surrender challenges, goals, and trials to Him.

If anything must consume us, He wants it to be Him. By relinquishing these earthly concerns to Him, we are able to conceptualize His attributes and will.

Sons and daughters of God must know that He is ready and willing to do a new thing in each of us. Trusting His resurrection power to revive us is not fruitless or futile. We attain the meaning of life when we allow the Life to fill us with hope, joy, and so much more. Death of a dream or relationship has lost its sting, because the Resurrection and Life prevails over it. With reverberation, depend on God for release and revival. There is nothing impossible for Him to perform. Giving every aspect of our life to The Life will affirm His Word to us, that *"we shall not die but live, and shall declare the works of God,"* Psalm 118:17.

Contaminated
Blood

lood is thicker than water is an old proverb dating back far beyond 1672. It means that one can expect more kindness from family than from strangers; family ties have claims that are universally acknowledged. Much to the dismay of many, this proverb has contributed to a considerable measure of dolorous individuals. An attestation of this 21st century reality is the capitalization of family issues by the electronic and print media. Ratings and sales ascend as families' personal dilemmas are exposed and exploited to households where viewers and readers possess dissimilar views of the family. Consequently, man's shifting beliefs and diverse interpretations have established warped ideas toward this support system. In many instances generations habitually advocate abuse and pursue perversion based on a mind-set. These generational attitudes have contributed immensely to the emotional scars and spiritual discord in many families.

For many, positive experiences have been localized or forestalled due to selfish expectations of kin. The likes of loyalty, conformity and fear in the bloodline have worked to frustrate the spiritual, emotional and intellectual development of family members. The very institution that God intended as a nurturing conduit is often filled with disapproval and denial towards true progression. Here members are ostracized, abandoned and ousted based upon righteous and unrighteous choices. Companionship, affirmation and tolerance are withheld to those who have done absolutely nothing deserving of mistreatment. Celebrating positive personal and family accomplishments are not the norm for many persons; rather hostility is. Such an environment is neither safe nor supportive. These descriptives are not rare, but real. Each serves as a reminder that Norman Rockwell's perspective on life is considerably distant from the realities of many a person.

Acknowledgment of such harsh realities can evoke discomfort in many individuals because they are not prepared to consider those whose history includes unpleasantries that are foreign to them. Detachment from this spiritual and societal problem has created a host of insensitive and uneducated individuals, to which neighbors, caregivers, spouses, friends and church members constitute.

Close observation will reveal that many individuals feel a strong sense of obligation to the family unit. This condition can be either impressive or oppressive. The latter is topical, for some persons accept a life of excessive subservience and emotional bondage within the family. They are unwilling to distance themselves from baseless relations because of their severe need to be affiliated and affirmed. Although a sense of belonging and need of approval are human characteristics, in the extreme they become insecurities and needless weights. Grievous, yet real, is that some abused and oppressed individuals find comfort in being victimized. In allowing deviant behaviors to be inflicted upon them they dismiss themselves from responsibilities that reflect strength, change and maturity. Although a corrupt concept, this type of environment is considered a comfort zone for those who refuse to mature holistically. It matters little to these individuals that there is an absence of agape love, trust and other salubrious components essential for strong and enduring relationships.

Those who truly love us allow and encourage us to develop and see God's promises fulfilled in our lives. When our families (biological and church) do not extend nurturing qualities to its members, we become candidates for self destructive behaviors. But thanks be to God who gives us the victory through our Lord Jesus Christ. Knowing our human frame, He provides replacements. Through them we can experience relationships full of agape love. During the process of our divine transformation, Jehova-jireh sends stand-ins to bless our lives. These special people possess the supernatural ability to nurture as God intended parents, grandparents, siblings and other relatives to. Christ has truly ordered events so that we do not have to live in self pity due to rejection, abandonment or misunderstanding.

We all need what Christ offers. He is aware of our social side; afterall, He made us and encourages socialization. To appease this need in us, our Creator places us among fellow believers who love and serve Him, thus establishing new and holy relationships. To add to our amazement, whatever we lacked in a particular biological relationship, our Heavenly Father provides in an ordained Christian union. Sensitivity, friendship; whatever we need God's got it.

In God's own time and unique way He places precious human jewels in our lives and us in theirs. Our kin are in the body of Jesus Christ. Receive them and be blessed. Simultaneously, our God establishes within us the special ability to parent a child, be a friend and other roles necessary for the blessing of other lives. We serve a loving and awesome Creator who is able to supply our every need.

God uses people as well as other sources to bless us. Let us embrace His love through them. Family members may not understand or accept the new found affection found in Christ and His people, but that is not a concern of God. God's plan should not be rejected because kinfolk have a problem with what God chooses to do for and through those who believe in Him. Our Eternal God knew us before and knows us better than anyone else, Psalm 139:1.

Still, for those who refuse to confront or separate from abusive kin because there is a desire to change them, know this, *the change may never come and we can not change people.* God alone can change the hearts and minds of people. He cares for each of us and desires that we accept His Son,

Jesus Christ. Through this acceptance we are changed into the individuals He finds favor in. Whether He desires to
change the situation or not, we must be willing to be changed
which gives Him the glory and us a testimony.

There are so many blessings to be found in family. Every
person who has benefited from true acts of love in their
family ought to thank God continually. Every relative who
has blessed our lives we ought to praise God for. However,
we must position and keep all things in proper perspective.
Relatives are not substitutes for Christ. It is God and God
alone who is to be worshipped and adored with all of our
heart, mind, and soul. Indeed kinship should not be a hindrance to experiencing God, *"He who loves [and takes more
pleasure in] father or mother more than [in] Me is not worthy of Me;
and he who loves [and takes more pleasure in] son or daughter more
than [in] Me is not worthy of Me,"* Matthew 10:37. Many people
have forfeited the greatest gift ever because of the opinions
and traditions of family. Their love is extended towards the
gift more the giver of the gift. Additionally, a substantial
number of Christians are midgets in the faith; unrooted in
the knowledge of Jesus Christ and clueless to the meaning of Christian service because of a sibling's self-serving
expectation. A child's and a parent's spiritual growth are
stunted because criticism, confrontation and change are
too much of a challenge to trust God for. For the well being
of our souls we must consider God's call and purpose for
us over other's expectations of us.

The child within each of us has retained some insecurity
born out of a negative experience. However, they should

not be given permission to consume our thoughts and order our steps. God loves us even if a loving close knit family is not a part of our history. Through Him we can move beyond the unpleasant phases of life. God has planned so much more for that rejected and abandoned person of yesteryear. He promised to be closer than a brother and that is pretty close, Proverbs 18:24. Furthermore, disappointment and heartbreak do not deserve the power to shackle anyone into a dysfunctional web and a sinister cycle of oppression. The absence of biological parents, lap chats, appropriate warm embraces or affirmations can not keep the Lord from loving and establishing His children. Neglect may have been commonplace for someone, but God sees each of us and knows our frame, Genesis 16:13 and Psalms 103:14. Memories of physical, sexual, mental and verbal mistreatment may consume the mind, but God knows our name as well as our pain. His healing hand is ready and willing to give and restore wholeness in our lives.

An aspect that is familiar to many families is the marking and mocking of an individual who is regarded by other family members as different. Whether the label is misfit, oddball, blacksheep or nonconformist this relative does not measure up to the standards set by his/her family. Sadder still is that many of these individuals believe the relentless lies; that they are a mistake instead of a miracle. None of us are mistakes and neither are we responsible for someone else's mistake in life. God has allowed us to come into this world. We have a purpose in life and the Creator has the blueprint for it. Albert Einstein said, "I shall never believe that God plays dice with the world."[1] I concur and submit that He does not play dice with us. None of us are here by the roll of the dice, luck, a big bang or man's evolutionary theory. We are seen and known by the Creator Himself. We must see and get to know Him. Only then will emptiness and addictive behaviors, which are sponsors of perversion, be replaced by the power of God. It is His will that each of us be saved. He is willing to embrace and empower us; the oppressed as well as the oppressor.

Just as clean blood and water are contributors to the good health of any individual, godly biological relations assist in the development of well rooted and established children of God. Contaminated blood does the body no good. In its polluted state it is nontransfusible and a threat to life. As contaminated blood threatens life, an unholy family works against abundant life. Infections, viruses and diseases travel through the blood robbing organs and other aspects of the body of strength. Imagine what happens to a family when sin is allowed to permeate and control it. The results can be deadly.

In the aforementioned proverb the word family represents blood and thickness signifies strength and security. Salubrious blood is comprised of essential elements and nutrients which sustain the entire body. When these provisions are neglected or continually replaced with junk foods, the body loses strength and the ability to perform the simplest of tasks. Comparatively, when families discard or substitute vital nutrients that are mandatory for their stability, weakness, deterioration and collapse are inevitable. A biological union that opposes peace, encouragement, holistic development and other essentials for godly character building is not in concordance with the plan of God. His plan embraces our spiritual commitment to Him and contribution to His cause. Living outside of this divine will is simply existing in a contaminated state. The converse to such a fixed state is living to the glory of God; giving our best to God and helping our kin to conceive and achieve the best for themselves. Families that exhibit such nurturing qualities towards its members are truly strong and secure.

Moreover, this form of strength and security does not establish perimeters which thwart personal identity and ideals. Such practices are neither commissioned or ordained by God. Parenthood and genealogy is not intended as a means of control and abuse. Incidentally, we need to be reminded that our children are not ours, they like us are God's creations. We must be ever mindful of what we do and say to them. Knowing that some sayings are embedded in our families and cultures, we ought to rethink and reword some things that we have heard and tend to repeat. No parent has the right to apply the saying, "I brought you into this world and I'll take you out of it." It is God who gives life and any human who desires to commit murder shall give an account before the Ultimate Judge. Parenthood is not a license to mistreat offspring. To do so is not without consequences. Parents are responsible for rearing children in the way of the Lord, Proverbs 22:6 and Ephesians 6:4, letting them see the Light of Christ at work in us.

Blood may be thicker than water, but obedience to Christ

is profitable, for in it is true strength and eternal security. Families must know that God is first, not the institution. We are gifts to one another; therefore, we should work to create environments that are conducive for each others' spiritual, emotional, intellectual, social and physical development. Contention, abrasiveness, apathy and hostility should not be ingredients of any family. If such forms of evil exist within the unit, the Lord will enable others outside of the family to love, righteously instruct, and encourage those whose family has lived outside of the will of God.

Although there is a satanic attack on the family, this gift of God does not have to be turned over to the perverted suggestions of wickedness. God has ordained the family unit, Genesis 2:22–24, and has called us into spiritual growth. As individuals and as family we can be who He has purposed us to be since through Him we can do all things. Thus, there is solace in knowing that God is able to cleanse, correct, and create families.

Our God is eternal, omnipresent, reliable and so much more. He tells us that He is closer than a brother, Proverbs 18:24b. We can count on Him being with us on earth as well as reigning with Him in Heaven. This kind of closeness and dependability families can not claim. If we must talk about blood and how strong it is, then let's talk about the blood of the Pure and Perfect One; the One who models how families ought to live and whose uncontaminated blood is powerful and pure enough to wash away all sins. Moreover, its cleansing power heals and closes all wounds never to be re-opened again. Christ's shed blood represents what families and every person ought to be. No family member can die for us. Surely none can save our soul from a burning hell, for it is through the blood of Christ Jesus that we have a way out of whatever sinful state we are in. Through His blood entire families are forgiven and cleansed of sins as well as bound in His love and strength.

Dysfunctional families do not have to be discarded, but rather entrusted to the One Who specializes in making the crooked straight, wrong right and contaminated clean.

Forgiveness Is
Not an Option

Somewhere, this very moment, someone is wrestling with a choice, to forgive or not to forgive. Whether it is beneficial to fight fire with fire, return evil for evil or to be good to the one who has offended them. In the battle between two wills, inflicting harm to an offender is a continual thought while praying for the salvation of the offender's soul is a thought far removed.

Because this is a period of distress, the distinctive qualities of a canker are working to establish residency in a believer's life. Someone is allowing the ordeal of impassive words or a reckless act to become an open wound filled with corruption and oozing with erosion. The result of their painful experience is responsible for emotional, psychological, and spiritual erosion. Sadder still is the ongoing anger that is socially erosive. The demonic influences operating in the saint's life impregnates the lives of others in his/her circle. Aware or oblivious of the believer's contention, relatives, friends, colleagues, neighbors, and strangers are subjected to demonic activity and influence when in the presence of this unforgiving person.

Like a cow chewing cud, this wounded individual mentally replays the incursion. Not letting go of the infraction allows memories of the incident to resurface automatically. These thoughts are always fresh and yes, in some instances, favored. This person prefers the notion of keeping the wound open rather than letting it go for often it is their license to act irresponsibly.

Somehow the belief is that the offense is reason to act unseemingly. Responsibility and accountability for acts of malice are out of the picture because oppressive and retaliative spirits have convinced the believer to accept such unordained roles as victim and avenger. Accepting the role of the Eumenides or sitting duck is not a part of God's plan for Christians. His plan and purpose for us is to be victors and overcomers. Moreover He has predetermined that vengeance is His and His alone.

Having been overcome by humiliations, violations, and other types of indignities, such persons have developed an attitude that signifies unnecessary suffering and unhappiness. Resentment has persuaded some to believe that they are actually hurting someone else when in reality they have imprisoned themselves. Getting a grip of oneself and moving on to higher heights in the Lord is not a part of this person's intention. Embracing the offense has placed them in irons.

Entrenchment of the forces of darkness is keeping a brother and sister in Christ, somewhere, bound and blind. The belief that they have every God-given right to act upon feelings such as anger and resentment, is an indication that they are allowing evil to overcome them. They do not see the need to overcome or, master evil with such qualities as goodness and peace. To many, overcoming the offenses with these refinements is seemingly preposterous.

Regardless of the range of negative feelings induced by offenses, it is ultimately our attitudinal and behavioral response to them that will either keep us from being blessed or bring the blessings on. Christ told us to, *"Let this same attitude and purpose and humble mind be in you which was in Christ Jesus:,"* Philippians 2:5. We are further reminded, *"When angry, do not sin; do not ever let your wrath last until the sun goes down,"* Ephesians 4:26. We are not responsible for what anyone else does or does not do; however, we are accountable and responsible for what we do and do not do.

As a result of a violation, someone is justifying, this very moment, their decision not to forgive another. "You don't know all that was done to me or said about me," are ringing out. However, having someone know the ends and outs of the matter does not help in our relationship with God. Yes God, the one who knew of the violation before you and I. And yes, the same God who commands his children to forgive that we may be forgiven by Him. God who instructs us to forgive seventy times seven, and to bless them who persecute us, who are cruel in their attitude toward us; bless and do not curse.

Recently I heard a politician say that his colleague did not have an option in deciding how to cast a vote. This statement confused me initially because the congressman seemingly did have a choice in the matter. But as I surveyed the intent of the speaker, I realized that he was making it very clear that if the congressman voted against the terms of his political party, the consequences for his decision would be considerable. In this instance consideration of long term effects were supposed to neutralize a possible choice. So too are believers in Christ reminded of future outcomes that hinge on current decisions.

The turning point for every believer should be wanting what God wants. To forgive or not to forgive is no longer a question. Following God's command to forgive is the right decision; a decision that the Lord will enable us to live with. It is important for every believer of the Lord Jesus Christ to know and understand the will of the Lord, for it is not His will for us to be ignorant, *"Therefore do not be vague and thoughtless and foolish, but understanding and firmly grasping what the will of the Lord is,"* Ephesians 5:17.

Christ's love pardons all of our sins and the sins of others, *"But God shows and clearly proves His own love for us by the fact that while we were still sinners, Christ died for us,"* Romans 5:8. We are not Christ, however, we have the Holy Spirit who enables us to do many things, one being, to forgive. It is the Holy Spirit that teaches us how to make room for someone else's mistakes, weakness, and sins.

For the select group who believe that forgiveness and

forgetfulness are impossible, they are in error. It is the Comforter who enables us to forgive and forget. Such a task is impossible for man, but not for God, Genesis 18:14, Matthew 19:26, and Luke 1:37. To even say that we can forgive and not forget is a fallacy, for children of God can do all things through Christ who gives us strength, Philippians 4:13. Forgiveness and forgetfulness are cut from the same mold. To forgive is to let go of all resentment and ill will towards a person and the offenses committed by that person towards us. Forgetting is not becoming amnesic, but rather it is relinquishment of unhealthy feelings and attitudes regarding our offenders and ourselves. Amnesia is a gap in or loss of one's memory due to shock, fatigue, brain injury, repression, or illness.

Divine forgetfulness on the other hand, involves intentional disregard of an offense and ceases to notice, give attention to, or remember the offense. Intentionality is key. We must want to move on, let go, and be at peace. Willingness to press forward is significant because the ungodly variables which influence the way we remember events can not stand against the mind that is under the authority of Jesus Christ. Choosing how we remember an offense can either make us sick or make us whole; therefore, follow through on each of these qualities is a preventive measure against enslavement to unsavory memories.

The Holy Spirit shows us several things about ourselves during the forgiveness process. Although we have been wounded, He shows us who we are and who we should strive to become. It is in these scenes that we see that if it had not been for the grace of God we could be in a worse state. Thus, to remember or hold on to someone's offenses is to continually see them through the eyes of the world and not of Christ. The Lord wants us to pray for them, instruct and encourage them in Him, and if possible, live peaceably with them, Romans 12:18. But above all He wants us to forgive them.

There are times when we should evaluate ourselves; question our agenda. Do we remember offenses to validate evil or promote righteousness? In our choice of remembering, are we seeking supporters to rally around our selfish cause? Do we fear the challenges of progression? Do we enjoy images of personal vengeance? If the offense hurt so bad, why revisit it over and over again? Is there some form of pleasure or satisfaction in the resurrection of pain and anger? God tells us to monitor our anger for a reason Ephesians 4:26. Retained anger only leads to vengeance, unforgiveness, and other sins. Also total recall and embracement of offenses towards us create a chasm between us and those dear to us. A time will come when associates and acquaintances will want us to relinquish the anger because of needless anxiety placed on us and our relationships. *"Cease from anger and forsake wrath; fret not yourself—it tends only to evildoing,"* Psalm 37:8. *"..., but he who harps on a matter separates even close friends,"* Proverbs 17:9.

Holding on to anger, resentment, and vengeance is desirable, but children of God really do not have a choice in this forgiveness business. Because we are of God, we are subject to the Truth and are held accountable for what we know to be true. God makes it very clear that sons and daughters of God are to forgive others of their offenses, debts, or trespasses against us. Like all of the Lords' commands, forgiveness is a medium of empowerment and freedom for the one offended. We are not enslaved to spirits that are adversarial to God's program, rather through forgiveness we are empowered to progress in the will of God.

It should be our desire to never find ourselves at this place again. Whatever the reason, we should challenge ourselves to think of offenses as testimonies in the waiting. Every time we revisit accounts of offensive experiences we should strongly consider how God has delivered us out of a dismal situation. Such reflective, yet controlled thinking is powerful, for it does not allow offenses to have the rule over us.

Trusting the Lord continually, will reveal how He turns reminders of personal abuse and violation into tools for our spiritual growth, and vehicles for praise, worship, thanksgiving, and testimonies. The Lord promised that all things work together for the good of them that love Him, Romans 8:28. Undoubtedly, casting the memory of an unwholesome experience on to the Lord guarantees spiritual healing. Surrender to God is not weakness, but strength. Casting any care onto the Lord assures that the strongman (specific demon that has established a stronghold in our lives) has nothing to use against us. What the Lord gives us through praise, worship, thanksgiving, testimonials, goodness, peace, prayer, and other weapons in His Holy arsenal fight mightily against the wiles of the devil; thus, diffusing any kind of demonic activity. God promises in II Corinthians 10:3–5 that He is able to destroy strongholds in our lives and do it in a way that the world and Satan can not copy and understand.

When we truly forgive, recollections of personal offenses are not granted authority to thwart God's plan for our spiritual development. Surrender of our pain and anger to the Lord disables the intentions of Satan. This salubrious choice makes room for us to be blessed in our meditative moments and diminishes the power that unwholesome experiences once had over us. Conversations from those who are responsible in some way for nurturing children, will attest that it is common for children to intentionally dismiss directions or instructions that are unfavorable to them. Selectively they remember and remind their care giver of something that supports their current interest. Similarly, believers can determine which memories are to be reserved and supportive towards our walk with Christ. Selective memory has benefits to the Christian when our perspective parallels that of Christ. We should not try to dismiss events of our past, but the outlook on them should be fresh. Forgetting those things that are behind, and reaching for what Christ has in store for us, Philippians 3:13 and no longer remembering or considering the things of the past because our God is about doing new things for us, Isaiah 43:18–19.

While the Lord desires that we be at peace with Him, ourselves, and others, the father of lies continually works to develop strategies that thwart this divine plan by using confusion and other agents of spiritual wickedness. Their assignments entail the prevention of spiritual prosperity in our lives. They work aggressively to keep offenses alive by tempting us to harbor them long enough to miss God's perfect peace and power. Yielding to such satanic tactics only place us in servitude to sin; all to Satan's delights.

Rulers of darkness know that if we permit the Holy Spirit to take care of our feelings connected to an offense, we will have a testimony that they can not fight against. To prevent testimony development, the devil instructs several of his followers to take up residency in our environments. There they battle against the purposes of our King. Speaking contrarily to His words and dismissing His works, the demonic medium labors vigorously to imprison us through various means.

Oftentimes we identify only the unforgiving spirit, which works to persuade us to decide against mercy and grace. How clueless we are to the other disciples of Satan that are responsible for grounding our decision not to forgive. I am continually learning that demons do not work alone. Like mice, if you see one there is another nearby. However, asking the Holy Spirit to identify them by name blows their cover. Using God's arsenal to confront them, frustrates their efforts and nullifies their work in our lives.

I have ascertained the names of several members of the demonic militia who have been assigned to visit me and even take up residency in my life. Although varied are their duties, their intent is to keep us from forgiving ourselves and others. I am confident that avoidance, spitefulness, faultfinder, bitterness, despondency, niggardliness, egoism, delusion, rebellion, and hostility, to name a few, are aggressively working today to torment the saints and create a spiritual chasm between God and mankind. But God in His goodness has provided a way for our victory. Knowing that we would not wrestle against flesh and blood, God prepared ways for us to fight. It is only through the use of His weapons that our victory over spiritual wickedness is guaranteed.

One subtle and crafty imp that troubles the spirit of an offended person is *avoidance*. It attempts to take authority in our lives by causing us to detach, retreat, or refrain from valuable relationships. Avoidance wants us to believe that no one can be trusted, not even God. According to this spirit, we need to abolish conversations and activities with others for we are better off left alone; alone where Satan and his disciples can have a field day with our minds. But God has established **confrontation** as a means to suppress this spirit that thrives in our misery, Matthew 18:15–18. When we have a divinely led face-off with our offender and/ or the memory of an offensive act, the intentions of God are clarified. For it is His will that we love Him with all of our being and others as ourselves. To love in these manners establish relationships that are spiritually healthy, mature, and prosperous.

Although the essentiality of relationships is true, we do not need to establish bonds with everyone. Every person that we come in contact with will not offer the witness that supports God's plan for our total development; therefore it is imperative that we know what and who God desires for us. Fear and other feelings may cause us to be evasive or withdrawn in relationships, but they are not representative of the fruit that Jesus intends to identify heirs of righteousness. Union with Him and His people result in love, power, and a well balanced mind. Divine confrontation is a pathway to such a harvest.

Another demonic missionary is *spite*. It persistently works to persuade us to harbor evil thoughts against others and to act on them. In this state we are capable of almost anything because such thinking and actions seem lawful or appropriate. To act on spite's report evidences our loss of control and its persuasive ability. **Kindness**; however, is a mighty eliminator and defusor of spite's intentions. Although to some this weapon typifies wimpishness, strength and effectiveness are its by products. When kindness is executed, people are led to repentance, Romans 2:4 and II Timothy 2:24–26. No wonder it is classified as a mighty weapon before God, II Corinthians 10:4. A passion of the physical person is evil for evil. But kindness operates out of the spiritual person. I view it as one of God's drawing cards. Instead of seeking revenge, we are expected to continue being holy vessels for supernatural experiences. Being kind to one who has wronged us is not natural, but it helps to lift Jesus. Through this supernatural act onlookers and us witness the saving and sanctifying power of God.

Spite operates outside the will of God by taking our focus off of Christ and onto our flesh. Kindness on the other hand draws the offense, the offender, and the offended one to the cross.

Faultfinder's instructions are to give unreasonable censure. When we listen to the report of this demon, we see little to no good in others particularly our offender. Being highly critical of others makes it difficult for us to extend mercy and to look beyond their faults. But a **patient** spirit focuses on the will of God for mankind, not desiring that any should perish, but that all should turn to repentance, II Peter 3:9. This divine trait sees hope and promise even in the vilest offender. Looking beyond imperfections and sin, patience holds our tongue and keeps us from acting unsuitably. Anxiety and other nagging spirits do not have the victory over us when patience is executed. Through it we shall win the true life of our souls, Luke 21:19.

The spirit of *bitterness* works to create an attitude of distrust and distress. Like the very memory of the taste of something bitter, this wicked spirit presents memories in such a way to cause emotional misery. If healing has not begun in one's life, bitterness uses the pain from the offense to help mount an attack on the personality. The individual becomes intensely unpleasant, antagonistic, and frigid. **Goodness** overpowers this demon because it is opposite in composition. It defies the rationale of bitterness and works to empower and heal the life of the offender as well as the one targeted by the offense. *"Do not let yourself be overcome by evil, but overcome evil with good,"* Romans 12:21.

Now *despondency's* assignment is to project thoughts of hopelessness. When we are emotionally and spiritually wounded what we do not need is to be told that we have no way out and that we are nothing. When we believe these lies, we have little to no reaction to the joys of life. Life has its dark side as well as its bright side. Despondency orchestrates lies and circumstances so that we never experience or appreciate the bright side of life. Even the dark side can be used to empower us, but this warrior of darkness would have us to remain in darkness. Satan has devised a strategy to thwart spiritual empowerment. He will do whatever it takes to keep us from knowing the power of God and applying His power in our lives.

As always God is right on time and ahead of the game. Being the all knowing God that He is, He has bestowed **hope** for His children. *"Such hope never disappoints or deludes or shames us, for God's love has been poured out in our hearts through the Holy Spirit Who has been given to us,"* Romans 5:5. Hope is merely desiring or longing for an expectancy; trusting and anticipating that something or someone will come through on our behalf. Despondency aims to short circuit any trust most of all trust in the Lord. This spirit does not want us to have anything as the center or focus of hope. A hopeless person is like the living dead. He or she does not see positivity in the future, present, or past. Nothing has worked, is working, or will work for their good. Hope changes such a mind-set. It is essential for living. Hope in God shows us the Way, assures Light at the end of the tunnel, declares freedom for all who know the Truth, and grants abundant and eternal Life to all who believe and trust in God.

The *niggard* spirit is simply stingy and unwilling to share oneself or possessions all because of a chip on the shoulder. Here again justification for not trusting others is displayed because of a wound. A few of the lies of this spirit are, *"There are no personal benefits in the giving of yourself or possessions. No one will appreciate your generosity anyway. In your giving you will be disappointed again."* God does not get the glory out of a stingy spirit, but rather when the spirit of **generosity** is at work in our lives. It is His desire that we share certain blessings with others. He gets the glory when we exercise generous and cheerful giving. Relunctancy in granting someone love, kindness, time, and other gifts that God has given to us, is of the flesh and works against God's purpose, II Corinthians 9:7–13.

Egoism's place in the scheme of wickedness advances lies. It says that no one cares enough about us and what has happened to us, so we must take care of ourselves. Take care of yourself for no one knows you better than you. Find your own way of dealing with the distress that this offense has caused you. You are important. Hey, even God says so. Do what is best for you. Forget about others and focus on you. These are all lies hatched from hell.

We should think of ourselves now and then, but when all we do is centered around self we have a problem. We are important in God's eyes, but we need Him more than us. Egoism blocks everybody out including the God who sees us; in the process persuading us to be independent and self sufficient. The weapon loosed by God in this battle is **trust**. The Lord tells us that sufficiency does not lie within us, but in Him, II Corinthians 3:5. When we stop seeing ourselves as "all that and some" and place that description on God, we are honoring Him as well as trusting Him for our very lives.

Being subject to God is acknowledging the truth that He is all in all and is the controlling factor of life, I Corinthians 15:28. Truly without Him we are nothing. We can not make this declaration if we see ourselves as everything or the one who can make things happen. Egoism deceives; directing the flesh to rely on the flesh. Trust in God reveals who we are and who God is. We need Him to forgive, heal, encourage, strengthen, and most of all save us. We can not do these things ourselves. Trusting in the Lord will reveal this fact to us.

Another ever present agent of evil is *delusion*. This spirit works persistently to make the lies of Satan believable by creating the impression that lies are our reality. The Lord confronts this demon with **Truth**. *"And you will know the Truth, and the Truth will set you free,"* John 8:32. Delusion goes beyond telling the lie, it sets the stage for visual effects. Any open vessel is used to propagate the lie. Children of God are called to walk by faith and not by sight; however, when we decide not to forgive, furtherance of disobedience is likely. You can be assured that walking by sight and not by faith is our lead for the day. And because the adage has been accepted, "I'll believe it when I see it," the believer is open for visual disception, set ups, and other forms of trickery devised by delusion. Consequently, Christ can use this adage to lead this deceived soul to the Truth.

Rebellion is another spirit hard at work. Defiant and out right resistant to God's command is its posture. Defy God to the point that coming back seems impossible. Rebellion is flat out contrary. Whatever God says just isn't accepted.

Nonetheless, **submission** loosed in Jesus' name will make this demon flee. The Holy Spirit says, *"So be subject to God. Resist the devil [stand firm against him], and he will flee from you."* Rebellion openly defies the authority of Christ. Submission silences rebellion's bark and smothers its flame of rage. According to the world submission is never a "good" word to use and being submissive to anyone is not appropriate in certain circles, but when applied to the Lord's principles for living, it is an empowering tool.

Anger is an operative element of unforgiveness. *"When angry do not sin; ...,"* Ephesians 4:26, we are told of God, but *hostility* has determined that there is reason to vent and that doing so is appropriate. Indeed we are due venting moments. However, acting on anger is what gets us in trouble. Being hostile to others because we are having a bad day is not always excusable.

Hostility is a member of violence's camp. When hostility is permitted to operate, eventually other members of its camp will show up in our life. Acts of violence usually are not far behind hostile remarks and/or body language.

Peace defuses the intentions of this demon. God's peace is so powerful that the Lord says it passes all understanding. Hostility can not tackle or shackle it because the Lord's peace is supernatural and eternal. The very quietness of peace is so powerful that the intentions of hostility can not ruffle our feathers when it is at work in us. Peace instructs us to speak softly, honestly, tactfully, confidently or not at all. Hostility urges us to speak or respond with a sharp and quick tongue, stabbing with every word. Peace directs us to be still. Hostility incites feelings of anxiety and impatience. With a sense of urgency we are to act now or say it now. Hostility thinks of itself as powerful and a defender of the vessel, but peace is not phased by all of that because peace is a defender of the feelings of a believer. It protects our feelings where hostility uses and abuses our feelings to ultimately destroy us.

When we are at peace with God, ourselves, our situations, and individuals, there is no weapon that is formed against us that can prosper. This perfect peace is not contingent upon someone being at peace with us. When we do our part to be peaceful with others, we are in line with the will of God our Father. Forgiveness is an act of love. Christ showed it towards us and we must do the same towards offenders in our lives. There may be those who reject our acts of love for various reasons, but we are called into a faith of obedience to God and not man. We are not responsible for someone else's actions, only our own.

The wisdom of God knows that through forgiveness we will be better conduits for His work and purposes. Man can not understand this thought of God. Thus, it is imperative that we obey God rather than man and allow our faith to rest in the wisdom and power of God alone. Refusal to forgive is a sin. Continuation to hold on to offenses is bondage. Choosing to walk wounded is representative of a walk in darkness. For the Children of Light, forgiveness is not an option. We are members of the faith that places emphasis on total obedience and dependence in Christ Jesus.

It is imperative that we trust the Lord for holistic healing, not the world. With its many mediums and mixed messages on healing, the world appears to possess resources beneficial to the mind, soul and spirit, but in actuality they drag us deeper into the pit of confusion and disobedience.

Forgiveness is God's prescription for healing. His restorative hand extends from our social to emotional self. It is prescribed for the troubled, perplexed, oppressed, dispirited, stubborn, arrogant, simple, affluent, and barbarized alike. It is His will that those enslaved by the aforementioned traits be released and prosper in Him spiritually. Giving Him the pain and shame of the experience assures results beyond our imagination, *"Now to Him Who, [by the action of His power that is at work within us], is able to carry out His purpose and do superabundantly, far over and above all that we dare ask or think infinitely beyond our highest prayers, desires, thoughts, hopes, or dreams,"* Ephesians 3:20.

In Him we have found the love that pardons and strengthens, as well as grace that covers all of our sins. Yes our sins. We need to stop focusing on what our offender did to us, but what we are doing. We are not accountable for the sins of others, we all have to answer for what we do and do not do. Getting the right perspective, letting the offense go, and permitting God to be Lord in our lives is essential for spiritual progression. Our relationship with God depends on these imperatives.

God promised to draw close to us when we cleanse our hands and purify our hearts from sin, James 4:8. Forgiveness is not an option for children of the Most High God. Through Him we can do all things and as He lived so are we expected to live. We can trust, love, forgive, endure, and excel. Because we are crucified with Him, it is no longer us who live, but Christ living in us and the life we now live in the body we live by faith in the Son of God, who loved us and gave Himself up for us, Galatians 2:20. Opting to dismiss the purpose of Christ in our lives through the retention of pain, grief, rage or any unhealthy emotion that stems from an offense, has both short and long range ramifications.

No emotion or incident should be given the authority to blind, consume, and lead us. Neither should the opinions of demonic agents be permitted to weave a web of lies. Everything that Satan and his cohorts tell us lack design for our betterment. All of their promises are empty because they do not own this world. Only God's promises are true. The earth is His and the fullness thereof. Even when spiritual wickedness devises strategies to make God's precious promises seem unrealistic and unreliable, His faithfulness prevails. He continues to save, forgive, and to perfect that which concerns us.

We are worshippers of the True and Living God, who has determined that we are more than conquerers and are doorways to Christ not doormats. Therefore, in the freedom that He has given us, opponents to our Christ are to be under our feet not the reverse. He has enabled us to stand in the liberty that He has given to us and desires that we do not return to the yoke of bondage, Galatians 5:1. Forgiving someone is indicative of God's love in us for His love enables us to forgive others of their trespasses against us. However, this great act of love does not mean that we continue to tolerate profane behaviors towards us, nor is it naiveté. Occasionally we will encounter individuals who view our forgiving spirit as weakness and a signal for them to conveniently practice the same ungodly acts towards us. Possibly they disregarded the fact that they experienced the power of God at work in us when we forgave them. Thus, we must continue to let them see God's powerful hand at work by standing firm to what is right by God and standing against that which is wrong. Avoiding issues and fearing rejection does not show the unbelieving and believing the capability of God's power.

For various reasons some tricks of the devil will get by us, so daily we ought to ask God to open our eyes to the chicanery of the enemy through others and circumstances. No one, relative, peer, sororal or fraternal acquaintance, official of any institution, is commissioned by our God to subtly or blatantly mistreat His people, *"Touch not my anointed ...,"* Psalm 105:15. Neither are we expected to permit others to disrespect the worth that God has instilled in each of us, *"Do not give that which is holy (the sacred thing) to the dogs, and do not throw your pearls before hogs, lest they trample upon them with their feet and turn and tear you in pieces,"* Matthew 7:6. Some people will never understand why we have released an offense and forgiven someone. To forgive may be considered foolish to them, but it is highly favored by God. For the unforgiving, pray for them and let them work through this stage of bondage. As for the forgiving crowd, continue to trust God and stand on His mandates for living. He does so much for us and others when we follow His way.

"Will I do your will?" is the question that God's people ought to continually ask themselves. It is a great substitute for the indecisive moments when forgiveness and unforgiveness compete to lead our will. Prayerfully the answer will always be "Yes, yes, yes Lord yes."

Give God All of the Glory

"Look at me I'm a testimony. I did not make it on my own, I'm not standing here alone. It was Jesus who gave me the opportunity. Look at me I'm a testimony."

The preceding expressions indicate that a Christian's life is a remarkable story; one worth sharing and examining. Both essential and common to every believer's story is Jesus, for He alone is responsible for our transformation and triumphs. Each account bears witness of God's matchless grace and power. Such accounts of what Christ did and does in our lives is a testimony. It is the victory story that Christ speaks of in Revelation 12:11; *"And they have overcome him by means of the blood of the Lamb and by the utterance of their testimony, for they did not love and cling to life even when faced with death."* When shared without shame and fear, these personal stories of victory in Jesus become weapons against spiritual opposition. Through them we are given the supernatural ability to overthrow and destroy strongholds and every lofty thing that sets itself up against the true knowledge of God, II Corinthians 10:3–6. Furthermore, they are tools for establishing righteousness in others as well as ourselves. No wonder Christ has assured us of victory over the world and the enemy, John 16:33 and Revelation 12:11. Truly they are awesome reminders of God's capabilities as well as His faithfulness. Greater still, are the ways that the Lord uses testimonies to convict, convert, and commit hearts to godliness. I am always amazed at how every experience in my life God has established as a testimony for my good and another person's blessing. I never know which testimony is next to be pulled out of my pocket when I am ministering because Christ has blessed me with many and more are in the making.

Knowing how relevant testimonies are to evangelism, it is sometimes annoying to hear testimonies that are pretentious or full of false humility, particularly during the devotional portion of a worship experience. Esteeming servant over Master is hazardous to the spirit. Capitalizing on the attentive ear of the saints just to get things off of one's chest or vent is poisonous as well. Such moments of selfish passion is misleading, to say the least, to those who need to hear how Christ can make a difference in their lives. Private or public credit to anything or anyone other than Christ for divine changes in our lives, is to err. Neglecting to give credit to the Holy One who gives good and perfect gifts is a grave mistake. Subsequently, using the forum of God's house to ramble on about Christless visions, flaunt affairs that are not Jesus centered, or read the church the riot act is simply dangerous business.

Our God works decently and orderly. It is His desire that we act accordingly as well. Going forward on our own, and expecting God's blessings on such fleshly statements as, "I am just going to say what is on my mind!" is not the Lord's way of glorifying Himself. He chooses to bless those seeking to worship, praise, and serve Him. When opportunists seek to get something off of their chests or stand in their own glory, God is not in it or pleased. It is not His will that Christian worship, praise and service be interrupted or oscillated by misguided individuals.

Because the Holy Spirit is a teacher, He will correct us and teach us all things. He chastens us always with a purpose of setting us on a righteous course. Case in point, His word purposes to encourage and build up His people. When we speak on our own and out of our flesh our words have the opposite effect of God's word. Our words become void and are discerned by the spiritually alert that empty utterances have gone forth. In addition, there is no spiritual fruit to evidence that what we have said or done is truly of the Lord.

However, when we speak under the direction of the Holy Spirit, our words are really God's words. They minister, heal, encourage, correct, and whatever else He deems essential for the listening ear. We see scripture come alive in such moments. The word of God says, *"His word does not return to*

Him void, but it shall accomplish that which He pleases and purposes, and it shall prosper in the thing for which it is sent, " Isaiah 55:11.

Who can know the mind of God? Before we stand and claim to speak for and about God, we should get insight from Him. Only then are we confident that God's purposes, not ours, are emitted. Having the floor during a testimonial should be a bold yet humbling experience. The Spirit of God in us should arise and our flesh abate. When we submit to God in the moment of testifying and expect Him to lead it, we can rest assured that He is glorified and well pleased with our declaration.

Hearing an angry voice or vain talk during testimonials can vex and confuse the human spirit. It is risky business pretending to stand on the name of God and deliver a personal agenda. In some instances, innocent ignorance is tolerable to a point, but every testifier must be aware that self-serving statements masquerading as spirituality are hazardous to the spiritually immature Christian and to the witness of the speaker.

Sadly, many churched individuals and Christians are unaware that they are not stating the impact Christ has made in their lives when standing to be a witness. A major contributor for error in such testimonials is that neither scripture nor the power of God is understood by the testifier, Matthew 22:29. Understanding scripture and God's power helps one realize that:

- Through Christ, not ourselves we can do all things, Philippians 4:13.

- Self-sufficiency is not to be glorified, but rather Christ's sufficiency, II Corinthians 3:4–5
- We all have sinned, none are righteous, our righteousness is compared to a filthy rag in God's eyes, and because of our sins Christ died, Romans 3:23, 3:10, Isaiah 64:6, and Romans 5:8.
- Through God's grace we are saved not of our finite abilities or anyone else's, Ephesians 2:8–9.
- The audience needs to hear about Christ and the gospel. How we synthesize the story with these essential elements makes the story personal and believable, Acts 26:4–23 and Acts 4:13–31.

Sharing what God has done in our own lives is a divine tool to win others to Christ. Talking about everything but His effect and impact on areas of our lives does nothing to draw others to the presence of the Most High God. He has to be lifted up that others may know Him, John 12:32.

Our very lifestyle in Christ is a testimony of what He continually does for those who abide in Him. Surely everyone who has accepted Christ as Lord and Savior has a testimony under his/her belt. Certainly through obedient living, Christians should have fresh accounts of how we know that God is real and that He lives within us. It is this knowledge of God that enables us to effectively tell others **our story** of the benefits of our fellowship with Jesus Christ. Knowing God personally also empowers us as we recount **His story**, the gospel. For children of the Living God are advised by Him to be ready to give an answer to anyone who asks us about our faith in Christ Jesus, I Peter 3:15.

Since our witness does not go unnoticed, we are responsible for our behaviors, attitudes and words. We are accountable to God for all that we do and think because we are not called into an aimless faith, but one of direction and purpose. Therefore, we should not be bound to lip service, but rather to the purposes of the Lord God, He who is and who was and who is to come, the Almighty, Revelation 1:8.

Comparatively, testimonies will differ. The differences work to establish believability and individuality. Some Christians think that drama should be a part of a testimony. The Holy Spirit has His way of making every testimony purposeful and powerful. Anyone willing to hear what God is doing and yearns for His truths will be blessed by both our profound and simple accounts. Through the Holy Spirit they are all genuine and effective. He promised that His word would not return void and would prosper where it is sent, Isaiah 55:11 and that if He were lifted up from the earth, He would draw people to Him, John 12:32.

The Lord draws us in His own way and how we respond and succumb to His drawing power varies. Our personality and life experiences play a significant role in Jesus' process for our renewal; therefore, our statement which reveals our life before Christ, how we came to Christ, and our present life in Him will differ from saint to saint. Praise God for our differences. For the differences in credible testimonies serve to validate His matchless attributes.

No one knows like we do what God has done for us. And when someone does something meaningful for us we ought to give them thanks. People of God can not thank God enough, afterall He gave His life for us. However, we can reciprocate the love by continually praising, thanking, worshipping, and serving Him. He did not stop loving us at Calvary, neither did His love cease upon His resurrection. His love is everlasting and it is active today. Continually God endows us with blessings beyond our asking and comprehension. Thus, we must continually give Him what He wants. He desires the glory out of our lives. We can not match God's love, but we can bless Him by allowing Him to have His way in our lives. In so doing we are used for a holy purpose. To be used by the Lord ultimately leads to testimonies that speak of the omnipotent God.

To God be the glory. Great things He has done and continues to do.

Mind Your Business

The Lord gives us so many blessings. With each comes responsibility, for everyone to whom much is given, of him shall much be required, Luke 12:48. The giver of every good and perfect gift expects us to be good stewards with each talent. We are to be productive (buying and selling) with each of His gifts until He comes, Luke 19:13. Every Christian has been assigned at least one task by the Father to help advance the gospel of Jesus Christ, for productivity is an essential part of our witness. Yet, for many in this great walk of faith there are questions about service which impede application of God's word and our spiritual gifts. Uncertainty is revealed when we ask—Why should I work for Christ? What is my calling? Where should I minister? When should I start my labor in Christ's vineyard? How will I build up believers of the Risen Lord?

Our God has an answer for all of our questions and is ready to address each of our concerns. However, before any of these questions can be answered we need a serious attitude; a spiritual attitude adjustment. Serving God without it is labor done in vain. The short, yet potent account of the woman with the interminable menstrual flow, Luke 8: 42–48, is one of many examples of what happens when our attitude about Christ is serious. This nameless woman went through twelve long years of being shackled by several weighty chains. Her issue of blood was not her only issue, for she was declassed, talked about, isolated, misdiagnosed and more. The physicians whom my sister paid and trusted to correct her disorder could not relate to her condition of humiliation. They were part of her male dominated society which had very limited views and use for its women. These men did not know what it was like to bleed from the body, moreover continually. They could not phantom the necessary routine for personal hygiene, neither the experience of continual pity and scourge. Could they possibly understand the hurt and embarrassment that followed her daily? I don't think so. Yet, without ceasing she exposed herself to their insensitivity and experimentation; all to rid herself of an uninterrupted flow of blood and to shake the stares of the people, stench and stigma.

Probably frail, friendless, and faint she endured the pushing, shoving, and harsh glares of the crowd for an encounter with Jesus. The reports of Christ's compassion and perfect medical record had reached her ears and she wanted to experience His works first hand. Consumed, but focused, nothing could stop her from muscling through the throng to one more occasion of hope. The bible says that she reached

Jesus and touched the edge of His clothes and immediately her flow of blood ceased. And Jesus knew that according to her confidence in Him, she had been strengthened and delivered by His goodness. With the crowd still close at hand God orchestrated events so that all of the people could witness His power, as well as bring the recipient of His goodness to a point of praise and service. She could have denied her involvement, but she came forward trembling. Falling before God she declared what he had done for her.

Unlike the woman with the interminable menstrual flow we need to hope in God first and foremost. Our trust in other things should not proceed trusting God. There is a familiar and misguided saying, "When all else fails trust God." This is such a contradiction to the word of God. We are to seek the Kingdom of God prior to seeking anything else. Even our attitude and works should be committed to Him, Matthew 6:33 and Psalm 36:5. Living obediently to these mandates prevent failures and usher in our successes. Next, we must be like the woman with the issue of blood in that we must push forward to experience God. When Jesus stimulates us by His word and works, we can strong-arm our way through the circumstances of life to encounter Him. Experiencing God will show us man's limitations and God's limitlessness. Knowing God will reveal woman's exhaustibility and God's inexhaustibility. Third we need to worship Him. My sister fell down before Him; she worshipped Him. Falling before Jesus is acknowledgment of who He is. When we experience God we can fall down before Him physically, mentally and spiritually. All that is within us will bless

Him. Such an approach to God is most definitely an act of obedience as well as an attitude that God can work with.

The woman with the issue of blood showed her love for God through a serious attitude. Privately and publicly she acknowledged His worth. *"Let this same attitude and purpose and humble mind be in you which was in Christ Jesus,"* Philippians 2:5. Her attitude led to her act of faith and these prerequisites led to her blessing. Although God used her approach and response to Jesus to create a teachable moment, He saw fit to esteem this woman for centuries to come. I can only imagine how she continued expressing her love for Him by allowing God to use her in service.

To adequately serve God in our works, we must have a mental and emotional position which regards the succeeding facts.

1) None of us can ever repay God for all that He has done for us.

2) God frees us from all forms of bondage.

3) God makes a way out of impossibilities.

4) God brings light to dark and dismal circumstances.

5) God permanently removes sorrow.

6) God gives hope for everyday.

7) God releases peace during our stormy seasons.

8) God furnishes us with strength when we are ineffective and tired.

9) God is faithful.

Certainly we can not operate or serve God in the anointing without knowing who God is and who we are. When we experience the various attributes of God we can not help but praise Him. Giving kudos to the Faithful One leads to honorable service; and surely when we *"roll our works upon the Lord [commit and trust them wholly to Him; He will cause our thoughts to become agreeable to His will, and] so shall our plans be established and succeed,"* Proverbs 16:3.

Indeed we must love God in order to adequately serve God. Our love is an attitude which develops into an action. Thinking of Him and keeping Him in remembrance makes us effective in His service. While working for God we should not compare ourselves to other laborers, and certainly we ought not compete with workers in the same vineyard, for neither comparison nor competition are of the Lord. The Holy Spirit does not compare or compete against Himself. Instead of wasting our time looking at what others are doing or not doing for Christ, we need to mind the business that God has assigned to us.

Jesus asked Simon Peter if he loved Him three times before His ascension into Heaven. Peter responded with a yes each time. After each of Peter's yes responses, Jesus gave him his assignment, *"Feed My lambs, Shepherd My sheep, and Feed My sheep,"* John 21:15–23. Once again we see where the love for God must proceed service. Surely Peter did not know God's blueprint for him, but he was open for the task set before him. Peter said something that is reflective of the thinking of many Christians today. He momentarily took his focus off of Jesus and placed it on another child of God.

"But Peter turned and saw the disciple whom Jesus loved, following the one who also had leaned back on His breast at the supper and had said, Lord who is it that is going to betray You?" When Peter saw him, he said to Jesus, *"Lord, what about this man?,"* John 21:20–21. It is understandable that Peter and the other disciple were close, homeboys; nonetheless, what his assignment was and what his friend's outcome would be should not have been a matter for his concern. Jesus let Peter know this by responding, *"If I want him to stay (survive, live) till I come, what is that to you? [What concern is it of yours?] You follow me!,"* John 21:22.

When we take our focus off of our divine assignment and mind the business of others we create the possibility of disorder which God is not a part of. I know that the bible says that Jesus showed Himself to the disciples on this occasion, but I can not verify who started the rumor that John would not see death. It could have been Peter, the other disciples, or John himself, but Jesus did not say that John would not die, the person not minding his own business did, John 21:23.

Peter witnessed much about the Messiah in his three year discipleship course. He truly had come to love the Lord. God had given Peter much and more was to come. Christ had modeled for him the true meaning and purpose of servanthood. He had been taught by the best servant ever that to whom much is given much is required; live so that men and women may see your good works and glorify God in heaven; do not let your good be evil spoken of; keep your lights trimmed and burning; and occupy till I come. He may not have known the extent of his assignment, but he knew that he had to be serious.

When our love for God is for real, nothing can separate us from His love; our flesh, bad days, addictions, absolutely nothing. *"For I am persuaded beyond doubt (am sure) that neither death nor life, nor angels nor principalities, nor things impending and threatening nor things to come, nor powers, nor height nor depth, nor anything else in all creation will be able to separate us from the love of God which is in Christ Jesus our Lord,"* Romans 8:38–39. Even when sin gets momentary victories in our lives, the love of Christ keeps us and enables us to continue working for Him, Romans 7:14–25. Paul had his faults and shortcomings, but God still used him for major ministry. God continued to work on the heart of this disciple because Paul loved Him with all of his heart, mind and soul. God is still working on hearts and developing minds bent towards Him.

Mary, the mother of Jesus Christ, is another disciple who loved God in her imperfectness. She was not chosen to be responsible in such a divine assignment frivolously. She was given serious attention. Her attitude for God and the things of God outweighed her imperfections. Often, like others, I wonder why God uses some Christians more than others. Since He has no respect of persons, what determined that Mary had what it took to accomplish her assignment and God's plan? My conclusion is threefold. First, I need to mind my own business. Second, Mary found favor with God because of her serious attitude. God entrusted her with much because He knew that she would convey also a godly response to her assignment. Her reaction to the prophecy is a witness and guide for present-day saints. Third, although our love for God, our faith in God, and His determination of our spiritual gifts are essential, He is sovereign. He can choose who He wants when He wants.

My "sister-friend" was ready; positioned to be blessed. Her serious attitude made her available for God's guidance and use, Luke 1:26–28. So many believers want to be used by God, but do not want to do what it takes to contribute to productivity in the Kingdom of God. When we are living the life that God instructs us to live, we find favor with Him. God's favor leads to blessings, and our blessings usher us to service. God blesses us because He is good and He blesses us that in and through our blessing we will serve and glorify Him.

Mary really had it goin' on. She was willing to act on God's charges. She was obedient without a complaint, *"... let it be done to me according to what you have said. And the angel left her,"* Luke 1:38. Like most children, many Christians follow the mandates of Christ with a grudging spirit. Pouts, complaints and reluctance best describe their response. God favors the heart that allows Him to do what He pleases with it. Mary did not have to be plodded along for she willingly welcomed the report of the Lord.

Mary was the type to respond to God's report with belief and praise. The bible says that even before the angel Gabriel departed, Mary blessed God by believing Him and praising Him. Her belief was later confirmed by her cousin Elizabeth's declaration, *"And blessed (happy, to be envied) is she who believed that there would be a fulfillment of the things that were spoken to her from the Lord,"* Luke 1:45. Mary also responds with verbal praise, *"My soul magnifies and extols the Lord. And my spirit rejoices in God my Savior...,"* Luke 1:46–55. Yes the Omniscient God knew that He could depend on Mary to give Him His kudos. She did not esteem herself, other people, or anything, but God. We can not adequately serve Adoni when He is not regarded as the only source of our energy and mission. Mary knew that she was not all that even after the realization that God had selected her for such a task. She kept the perspective of a servant. Such a perspective does not interfere with God's plan, but rather glories He That Is.

Another noteworthy aspect of Mary's persona is her intention to hold on to God's report. God entrusted her with much because He knew that she would weigh what He said. *"But Mary was keeping within herself all these things (sayings), weighing and pondering them in her heart,"* Luke 2:19 and *"... and His mother kept and closely and persistently guarded all these things in her heart,"* Luke 2:51. She was not like those who hear the word of God, get excited by it, but do not preserve it. She preserved His words so that later they would multiply in her life. It took time, but she saw the Word of God become reality. Through the birth, life, and death of Jesus, Mary saw God's report come to fruition. She may have wrestled with doubt, inferiority, and other antagonistic forces, but remaining in the Word increased her witness. Meditating on God's words empowered her. Through spiritual empowerment she could handle ridicule, scandal and more. Only through such power could she continue serving God.

Many of today's believers can identify with the love that Peter, Paul and Mary had for Christ. We too love God with all of our heart, soul and strength, Deuteronomy 6:5. Yet, occasionally we get side tracked. For one reason or another we lose focus of our assignment. Distractions arise which intend to prevent God's business from prospering. It is during these times that we should look to the only one who handled diversions well. He remained focused on His Father's business throughout His entire life. Set up after set up, He directed His actions and thoughts to the present and future pursuits of Kingdom building. Our Savior knew that in modeling servitude; minding the business of God, He was teaching us how to prepare for eternity.

The enemy of God has learned much about the results of Christian employment. For centuries he has watched how people of God have become empowered, confident and delivered through continued Christian service. It is this powerful witness that attracts people to God. Thus, it should be an expectation that the father of lies, the thief, would come to distort and disturb our view of servanthood. He wants to immobilize us in service and persuade us to abandon ministry. Through his deceptive devices we may become convinced that we need a break from it all because the task is overwhelming and exacting. However, such a break can be hazardous to our spiritual health.

When the Lord directs us into an area of service, He also gives us a burden for the people to be served. In our unauthorized leave of absence we carry that burden. We may try to deny our resignation, but the weight of the burden will not leave us because God's business has not been accomplished through us. God has His finger on us and He has ordained that we perform specific tasks. For us to oppose and reject his directives for us is simply dangerous. No one knows like us the impressions that the Holy Spirit has placed on our heart. Disobedience towards His instructions create a void in our lives and a mind-set which justifies our absence. Trying to conceal our interests and concerns for our area of ministry is simply a miserable feeling. The energy that it takes to rationalize our disobedience could well be spent serving our God. The Holy Spirit will not let us forget God's mission for us. Like Jonah we can not escape it. Unless we accept the will of God, we will not know perfect peace. Indeed the price we pay for stepping out on God is not worth the inescapable torment.

Christian service is fulfilling, yet draining. Why else would Christ tell us that the harvest is plenteous, but few are the laborers? It is during the demanding times of service that we are susceptible to the report and advice of the enemy. Of course anything that he says is born out of deceit. He is likely to tell us that our labor is a waste of time; that no one takes us seriously, and we need to take a break from it all. Even in the Christian community there are believers who do not regard our Christian service for they are those who place limits on what they will do for God. These individuals do not understand why other saints are still working when they are not. They usually rationalize why laborers ought to vacation or do something else, which is a diversion from God's plan. They may not always see themselves as a force of interruption and diversion, but they are. They perceive our responsibilities as just a bit much or going over board. They can be heard saying, "You don't need to do all of that."

Experiencing the lack of understanding and support for our divine vocation regretfully is par for the course. As misunderstanding and nonsupport shadowed Jesus' ministry, so to shall we contend with these adversaries. Nonetheless, we ought to remain focused on what God tells us. Through such obedience we shall increase in wisdom and find favor with God, Luke 2:49–52. Choosing to believe the words of Christ rather than the report of Satan will enlarge our faith in God and expand our ministries. We will be revived and encouraged by the greatest servant who ever lived. He alone will motivate us to continue the work in spite of what we see and do not see. Continually He proves to us that total reliance in Him is profitable—*"In all labor there is profit"* Proverbs 14:23.

Yes, the load does get heavy, but laborers ought to cast their cares on the one who said that His yoke is easy. We know what God has told us to do. When it is time to rest or move on into something else, He will create the moment. And what I have learned is that in the season of rest not only are we revived, but we are prepped for new business. Yes, there is always something to do for Christ when we are romancing Him. Even when we are away from it all, the seed of the assignment is within us. We may want to detach ourselves from the pace and pressures of the business, but what God spoke into our spirit will not leave us. Like fire shut up in our bones, we have to go forth with what the

Lord has laid on our heart—*"If I say, I will not make mention of the [the Lord] or speak any more in His name, in my mind and heart it is as if there were a burning fire shut up in my bones. And I am weary of enduring and holding it in: I cannot [contain it any longer],"* Jeremiah 20:9.

Another facet of our lives is the multiplicity of responsibilities. The thought of daily and weekly agendas can be overwhelming for the saints who wear many hats. Yet, for those who God has entrusted much, He expects complete dependence in Him. Through our continual trust in Him each task will be prioritized and prospered. It may not make sense to us why God even expects us to accomplish so much, afterall we are only human, but being the All Knowing God that He is, we can do all things through Him, Philippians 4:13. Surely total trust in Him and not our understanding will magnificently change our fretful perspective and course of life, Proverbs 3:5–6.

Periodically our calling may appear fruitless, inconvenient, and/or unmanageable. But things are not always what they appear to be. Actually whatever God has His hand in blossoms and is regulated. Although trying, genuine labor for Him is always encouraged and rewarded—*"They who sow in tears shall reap in joy and singing"*—Psalm 126:5 and *"But those who wait for the Lord [who expect, look for, and hope in Him] shall change and renew their strength and power; they shall lift their wings and [mount up to the sun]; they shall run and not be weary, they shall walk and not faint or become tired,"* Isaiah 40:31. We are encouraged further by the word of God in I Corinthians 15:58, *"Therefore my beloved brethren, be firm (steadfast), immovable, always abounding in the work of the Lord [always being superior, excelling, doing more than enough in the service of the Lord], knowing and being continually aware that your labor in the Lord is not futile [it is never wasted or to no purpose."* Surely Christ wants us to know that only what we do for Him endures and matters.

Continued focus on the purpose of our office is key. Vacillation will not lead lost souls to Jesus Christ neither will it contribute to our spiritual maturity. In all honesty, becoming and remaining centered on divine business is not effortless. There are a myriad of events that have the potential to distract us and hold our attention. They have the potential to persuade us to get caught up in our surroundings and not our Savior. Like Peter we may find ourselves telling God that we love Him, hear His response and then quickly devote our attention to something else—*"Lord, you know everything; You know that I love You. Jesus said to him, Feed My sheep. But Peter turned and saw the disciple whom Jesus loved, following-the one who also had leaned back on His breast at the supper and had said, Lord, who is it that is going to betray You? When Peter saw him, he said to Jesus, Lord, what about this man?"*—John 21:17, 20 and 21.

Not giving God our undivided attention can be costly, for inattentiveness allows misunderstanding and mistakes to weave their web of troubles into our lives. Remaining focused on God and the things of God is a difficult not an impossible mission. The Holy Spirit will order our thoughts if we let Him. He will tell us what is necessary and what only appears necessary. Through Him we will learn what obligations are self directed, world imposed or God led. I am reminded that not by might, nor by power, but by His Spirit God will enable us to mind His business, Zechariah 4:6.

As Jesus remained centered on the Father's business, those of us who are called and chosen by Him must also mind His business. God's business becomes our business when we remain in Him and He in us. Nothing ought to be given the authority to divert our purpose and discourage our calling in Christ. Like a business, we should be buying and selling, making use of the gifts and talents that God has given to each of us. The line of work in which God has called us into ought to be prosperous. Evidence of our prosperity will be in our commitment to Jesus Christ. Through our behavioral and verbal witness lives will be changed for the better because we have allowed God to work through us.

God is truly amazing. He honors our faithfulness and accepts our flaws. Mindful that His servants will be tempted, He has provided a way of escape. Knowing that we will sin, He is prepared to forgive and guide. We may have our doubts about ministry and even stray from His course, but God is able to move us onward. When we repent He pours out blessings too numerous to number. He then uses our experiences of waywardness and rebellion to work towards our good. Yes, even our disobedient acts are contributors to our empowered state. *"We are assured and know that [God being a partner in their labor] all things work together and are [fitting into a plan] for good to and for those who love God and are called according to [His] design and purpose,"* Romans 8:28.

God does not change, but He changes things. He is the God of opportunities, fresh starts and progress. He does a new thing through us when we repent. Whatever prevented us from previously serving Him holistically is discredited and discharged. With the absence of a resistant spirit, we serve God with more power and passion than before. He permits our new attitude to accompany our previous assignment. It is this attitude adjustment that enables us to minister to God's people and to help spread the precious gospel of Jesus Christ.

To the glory of God, those things that limited and confused us, no longer do. God has made all things not only work towards our good, but new. *"And He Who is seated on the throne said, See! I make all things new"]*, Revelation 21:5a. *["Do not [earnestly] remember the former things; neither consider the things of old. Behold, I am doing a new thing!"* Isaiah 43:18–19.

Hence, God restores and renews His servants. At such times we should position ourselves to have our minds blown by His awesomeness. As our parents and grandparents stood in awe as He showed them how to stretch their pennies, we too marvel at His supremacy as He shows us how to use our gifts. As He fed over 5,000 people on two different occasions, He is able to multiply the effectiveness of each of our talents. How can we not serve the Perfect God who gives so much to imperfect people?

With our love and attitude we can focus on God and the work of God. Our allegiance to Him guarantees success in our vocation and contentment in our spirit. No, we can never repay what Christ has done for us, but we can surely obey His commands. To sway in any direction other than the directive of Christ is sheer disobedience. For what we do not allow God to develop in us and bless others with, He takes away. Yes, in examining our stewardship over His gifts, He will take away the talent or gift that is inactive. He is not an Indian Giver, but the Father of good and perfect gifts intends to bring glory to Himself.

If we buy and sell, make use of each talent and gift, He will reward our faithfulness and initiative. Obedience with our responsibilities will result in entrustment of fresh talents and duties to be used in very unique ways. We may compare and critique the ministries of others, but what really is our point? We may find variation in assignments, what really is our intention? God has given every believer much to accomplish through Him; therefore, we really do not have time to question the assignments of others. We should be occupied with the particulars of God's business for us. So involved in His business should we be that when others think or speak of us our Christian service will be at the forefront of their thought and conversation. When persons look for us it should be understood that we are about our Father's business, Luke 2:49. Turning, even for a moment, to wonder about the role and mission of others in the Kingdom can tempt us to speak against God's call to others and ourselves. It is to our benefit to heed and focus on God's word, *"Follow me."* Indeed, being about His business ensures that we are in line with His will. Through such an assurance we do not have to deal with God or others telling us to mind our business.

I've Got to Tell It

"And you He made alive, when you were dead by your trespasses and sins. In which at one time you walked habitually. You were following the course and fashion of this world, were under the sway of the tendency of this present age, following the prince of the power of the air. You were obedient to and under the control of the demon spirit that still constantly works in the sons of disobedience, the careless, the rebellious, and the unbelieving, who go against the purposes of God. Among these we as well as you once lived and conducted ourselves in the passions of our flesh; our behavior governed by our corrupt and sensual nature, obeying the impulses of the flesh, and the thoughts of the mind, our cravings dictated by our senses and our dark imaginings. We were then by nature children of God's wrath and heirs of His indignation, like the rest of mankind. But God, so rich is He in His mercy! Because of and in order to satisfy the great and wonderful and intense love with which He *loved us, even when we were dead by our own shortcomings and trespasses, He made us alive together in fellowship and in union with Christ; He gave us the very life of Christ Himself, the same new life with which He quickened Him, for it is by grace that you are saved. And He raised us up together with Him and made us sit down together giving us joint seating with Him in the heavenly sphere by virtue of our being in Christ Jesus."* Ephesians 2:1–6

"Let the redeemed of the Lord say so, whom He has delivered from the hand of the adversary." Psalm 107:2

I just have to testify of what God's love has done for me. When I reflect on all of the phases of my life, I know that only Jesus arranged and orchestrated events in my life that have given Him the glory and worked for my good. This acknowledgment was not always a part of my mind-set. I have learned that telling how Christ makes a difference in our life contributes to spiritual healing and maturity.

Christians must openly acknowledge the benefits given to us by our Heavenly Creator and declare how His truths impact our lives. In doing so, we give Him all of the glory and praise. To give tribute to our Savior and Lord in this manner is an expression of our love, adoration, acceptance and obedience to the only One deserving of the highest praise. This kind of praise is reserved for none other, but the One who has made impossibilities possible, kept some events from befalling us, yet allowed some events to transpire that they would assist in character building. He has motivated us to accomplish multiple and superior tasks, given us peace in the midst of turbulence, instilled patience when anxiety demanded authority over us, and implanted divine visions to combat hopelessness and insecurity.

Occasionally some individuals assert their presumptions that life for me as a pastor's wife is a horrific experience. Without me asking for their opinions they impose their views of what they assume my world to be. They do not know that it is the presence and prerogative of the Holy Spirit that enables me to be the woman that God has called me to be. Being that woman has made me accountable to Him for several assignments. Existing as a pastor's wife and beyond that, Carl's wife are aspects of my life that I do not allow to define me, but rather are posts where I continually seek God for direction. All of my responsibilities need His guidance for without His hand in every area of my life, deterioration and insufficiency are imminent. I also realize that every divine post and gift needs my commitment because each will ultimately contribute to a fresh testimony.

The way that God has changed my life undoubtedly evidences His love for me. He has affirmed time and time again who I am in Him. I know that He loves me. I also know that my love for Him has to be demonstrated in several ways; one being the announcement of His involvement in my life. He does not want to be my secret love, but insists that I publicize our relationship. He is my everlasting love and thrill of a lifetime. Romancing Him is a delight for I have never known a love like this. In our relationship He frequently reminds me that without Him I am nothing, but because of Him I am somebody. Coming from Christ, this statement is acceptable; coming from any other source, it is not.

As much as I dream and value the affections of people, I recognize that my love for Christ must continually outweigh my desires, aspirations and human relationships. God has not given to me all that I want, but He has given me much. I know that if it were not for His mercy and grace, I could be a dead, demoralized, detained or deranged person. Life has not always been kind to me, but God knowing His purpose for me, has seen fit to let none of these things be.

I will praise His name forever because He has made me alive in Christ Jesus. Surely He has delivered me and set me apart for His business. For such an accomplishment, I am stirred in my spirit to tell others of Him and His abilities. Psalm 147:1 is a reminder that speaking of God's goodness is acceptable. It is pleasing and so beautiful to God. Simultaneously, it gives power and peace to the testifier. Communion with the Lord has taught me that it is good for my spiritual development to testify during a stormy phase in life and not give in to forces that resist God's purpose. Compliance to the Lord's instruction affords me His joy, peace and much more.

Our testimonials are spiritual weapons that withstand the demons of doubt, depression, confusion, and a host of other opposing potencies that want authority over us. Each testimonial validates the psalmist's stance, *"His praise will continually be in my mouth,"* Psalm 34:1. Such a position intends that we praise God not just for His blessings towards us, but for who He is and what He accomplishes through us for His sake. Such power and magnificence ultimately helps us to see clearly Him Who is, Who was, and Who is to come, Revelation 1:8.

Testimonies release the effects that burdens place on us. Situations that once appeared overwhelming and mountainous become minimal. Worry warts can attest that they became warriors when they gave Spirit led declarations of God's power and mercy. Yes, through testimonies the Lord shows us that we are more than conquerors. Through this godly tool, the testifier is lifted higher and used to leave hope to the listening ear. Spiritual health and healing takes place on both the receiving and delivering end. Thus, our testimony should not be a silent or passive acknowledgment of God's love and mercy towards us, but rather a consistent, vibrant, verbal and behavioral assertion that God changed us and is continually working on our persona.

God so loved us that He gave us His Son, the Holy Spirit, and principles to live by. His acts of love towards us may be resisted, but they are real. Acceptance of His love for us should provoke a vigorous response to testify of what His love has done for us. Every way He has made for us, is a testimony of His love and every promise kept is proof of His faithfulness.

Just as a testifier is expected to speak the truth by declaring facts germane to a court case, so to must children of God declare to the world what God has done, is doing and promises to do. We have been blessed of God; the testimony is a result of that. Sharing our testimony strengthens others as well as ourselves. Fear, nervousness, and forms of insecurity should not prevent us from strengthening our brothers and sisters in Christ as well as encouraging ourselves in the faith. We can do all things through Christ which strengthens us, Philippians 4:13, and that includes testifying. We may not fully comprehend the benefits that have been given to others when we share our godly experiences with them, but our sharing is truly an act of love and obedience.

Testimonies do not have to be unfamiliar or even redundant to children of the King because God has done so much for us. Walking with the Lord gives the child of God fresh and firm testimonies that help in kingdom building. It is through these testimonies, that we are able to triumph in and tolerate every test, trial, and temptation. Not only have we overcome Satan by the blood of Jesus, but also by the utterance of our testimony ... Revelation 12:11. We must tell our stories for our victories and other's hope in God.

Acknowledge and speak of God's presence and power in your life. Tell it, tell it, tell it. Tell it everywhere you go.

Epilogue

Satan tries to keep us from committing to a lifestyle of reliance in God, but accepting Jesus Christ is the most important decision that anyone can ever make. No, life will not be without temptations and disappointments, but its hard knocks work to establish our strength and stability. Life is not bland, but full and exciting for the believer of Jesus Christ because He uses both the winter and summer seasons of our lives to work towards our development and progress. Yes, every occasion in life benefits us. This is one reason why we ought to thank God in all occurrences.

Great is the Lord's faithfulness towards those who worship Him in spirit and in truth. It is He who inspires, empowers and improves us. It is His intention to do so. He will never give up on us. Working to bring to full completion the good work that He started in us in His will. Our feelings, friends and family may deny His presence and purpose for us, but

God remains focused and faithful inspite of humanity's understanding and doings. He has put so much before us; therefore, during seasons of testing and tribulation we need to ask the Holy Spirit to bring to our remembrance all that He has shared with us.

Believe, grasp, and proclaim the faith of unimaginable power and love. Endure and withstand each trial, knowing that in Him is strength, understanding, wisdom, hope and victory. As Jesus is allowed to be Savior so to must we permit Him to be Lord in our lives. Living so will reflect an attitude that God is enough. When He is not our all or our satisfaction, feelings, circumstances, and ungodly reports will consume us. Therefore, we should not resist Him, but rather fight human reasoning and the devil's rationale.

Our Lord did not look beyond our faults for nothing, neither are we His afterthought. He has put so much in us. There is so much to us than meets the eye. We must permit Him to show us and the world who He is through the episodes of our lives.

Retraction and resignation of the faith is never advantageous to Christians and fear of the unknown is not of God. Life may deal us merciless acts, but that is not cause to quit believing in God. Remaining in Him enables us to move beyond any point of pain and get over any adversity. Even after our victories, we must be ready to proceed. Onward, upward our directives in Christ keeps us on the move.

Our continued belief in God will allow Him to do a perfect work in us. In maturing us, others will stand in awe of

His wonders. They will be subject to His excellence when they look on us and hear of our experiences with and without Him. Through us others will see His keeping power. I am a witness that God does preserve His people, for I once endorsed a lifestyle that accelerated the aging process. But God protected, preserved, and positioned me for such a time as this.

Life in foster care, the projects and without the presence of a biological father has not left me bitter or broken. Rather God preserved me and uses my experiences to work towards my development and the good of others. While places where I have been and acts which I have partaken in have not always been wholesome, God has seen fit to preserve me still.

About nine years ago my driver side front window was shattered by a stray bullet as I drove to an evening worship service. The Lord orchestrated events so that neither my passengers or myself were wounded. With the bullet never found and the police astounded, the Lord was lifted up for He alone preserved us. He has not permitted the evil intentions of Satan nor the ungodly motives of certain individuals to reduce, persuade, hinder or embarrass me, because even in my imperfectness, I have chosen to live in integrity and uprightness, Psalm 25:21. I know that I am not the only testimony of God's keeping power since He does not have respect of persons.

God will keep us even when we do not want to be kept. His love towards us overpowers perplexity and frustration which are found in our trials. He did not ordain these powers to be conquers, rather we are. Through Him we have been guaranteed prosperity and triumph in every occasion in life. Indeed, we can make it and succeed in a manner that pleases the Lord.

What's next? Only God knows. Where do we go from here? Wherever Jesus leads us. Abandoning the faith, ministry or any responsibility that God has led us into is not His way. There is so much to learn by remaining in Him. Abandonment will work to prevent us from experiencing what God has in store for us. It intends to keep us from seeing what the end will be. The Holy Comforter tells us that our end of an episode is so much better than our beginning.

Don't quit on God. Hang in there. Stick it out. The benefits are worth it. Be teachable and patient for another testimony is on the horizon. Let Him be your portion. Yes, let Him be enough. Remain in Christ and put your expectation in Him only. He will come through for you.

Notes

Life for the Living Dead

1. "God helps them that help themselves" Familiar Quotations, John Bartlett (Boston, Toronto and London: Little, Brown and Company, 1992), 309, citing Benjamin Franklin, Poor Richard's Almanac, (May 1733).

Contaminated Blood

1. "I shall never believe that God plays dice with the world" Familiar Quotations, John Bartlett (Boston, Toronto and London: Little, Brown and Company, 1992), 636 citing Philipp Frank, Einstein, His Life and Times, (1947).

Order Form

To order additional copies of *Conversations With The King*, complete the order blank and forward it along with your payment to:

> Stephannie Solomon
> P.O. Box 3025
> Baltimore, MD 21229

Payment in the form of check or money order should be payable to the author and include $1.25 to cover shipping expense.

- -

(Please Print)

_____
Name

_____
Address

_____
City   State   Zip

_____   _____
Home Phone   Day Phone

# of Ordered Books	Book Cost ($12.00 each)	Shipping/ Handling	Total Cost

Order Form

To order additional copies of *Conversations With The King*, complete the order blank and forward it along with your payment to:

Stephannie Solomon
P.O. Box 3025
Baltimore, MD 21229

Payment in the form of check or money order should be payable to the author and include $1.25 to cover shipping expense.

(Please Print)

_____
Name

_____
Address

_____
City   State   Zip

_____   _____
Home Phone   Day Phone

# of Ordered Books	Book Cost ($12.00 each)	Shipping/ Handling	Total Cost